Hibiscus

LOPÈ ARIYO

For my mother,
the woman who gave me the tools, space and encouragement to dream and create
(even if you didn't initially agree with the food I conjured up)

HarperCollins*Publishers*
1 London Bridge Street
London SE1 9GF

www.harpercollins.co.uk

First published by HarperCollins*Publishers* 2017

13 5 7 9 10 8 6 4 2

Text © Lopè Ariyo 2017
Photography © Ellis Parrinder 2017

Lopè Ariyo asserts the moral right to be identified as the author of this work

A catalogue record of this book is available from the British Library

ISBN 978-0-00-822538-4

Food styling: Laurie Perry
Prop styling: Hannah Wilkinson

Printed and bound in China

MIX
Paper from
responsible sources
FSC www.fsc.org **FSC™ C007454**

FSC is a non-profit international organization established to promote the responsible
management of the world's forests. Products carrying the FSC label are independently certified
to assure consumers that they come from forests that are managed to meet the social, economic
and ecological needs of present and future generations, and other controlled sources.

Find out more about HarperCollins and the environment at
www.harpercollins.co.uk/green

LOPÈ ARIYO

Hibiscus

HarperCollins*Publishers*

Contents

INTRODUCTION

My experiences from childhood, school and university have shaped the way I cook and my food has become an expression of who I am. Born and raised in London, I have very early memories of taking trips to Brixton or Croydon market with my mother, Debbie, on Saturdays. We would always visit the vegetable stalls first, followed by the meat and fish stalls where I would do my best to hold my breath for as long as I could. The market was always so congested that I stayed glued to my mother for fear that I would get lost. When we got back home, I would help out in the kitchen as she prepared something like tomato stew or okra soup. I can vividly recall my mother blending and frying the tomatoes, finely chopping the okra and pounding ground rice in hot water with a wooden spoon. The splashes of tomato juice would trickle down the tiles as the stew boiled aggressively, the stove would sizzle as some of the okra soup escaped the pot and, to the delight of my nose, the smell of caramelized chicken crept slowly from the oven. Her approach to cooking has always been to create dishes that are quick and easy. This weekend ritual provided my first experiences of Nigerian cooking.

My mother raised me to be hardworking, honest and independent, and she also thought it was important for me to learn about my Nigerian roots and to connect with my extended family and culture. So in 2003, I went to an all-girls boarding school in Lagos, Nigeria. Initially it was daunting, but as I made friends and got into the routine, I became more open to the Lagos way of life. I came back to London for secondary school, bringing with me a strong sense of culture, solid friendships and an enriched appreciation of Nigerian food. I started cooking more and more, alternating between British and Nigerian meals to keep my cravings for the aromatic flavours to which I'd become accustomed at bay. I would mimic the dishes of beans and plantains or yam and spicy tomato stew that we were served at boarding school – simple dishes that were perfect for weekdays.

I met my closest friends in the sixth form and during our free periods, we would go to the shop to buy sandwiches, Scotch eggs, sausage rolls, cakes and elderflower and blackcurrant cordials to have mini picnics. Since not one of us had the same ethnic background, we'd always bring a dish that represented our own cultural history, too. We taught each other about ingredients and introduced each other to new flavours, and I discovered how joyful it was to invite them over and cook for them. This was one of the things I missed most when I first went to university. When I rang home, my mother would usually ask 'Have you eaten?' or 'Are you hungry?', as is the norm with most West African parents when their children are sad or moody. I found solace from homesickness in the kitchen and soon my housemates, who knew little about Nigerian culture, came to rely on me for ingredient and spice suggestions. We ended up cooking meals together, whether British, Nigerian or a mix of both cuisines. I realized that in the kitchen I was able to create a home away from home, no matter where I was.

For me, British and Nigerian influences are equally important – I like to merge the best aspects of both. I love the combinations of ingredients (especially the spices) used in Nigeria and West Africa, whereas British or European cooking tends to offer more time-effective methods. I am passionate about West African food because it promotes the use of fresh, natural ingredients and the emphasis is on taking care of your body without overthinking things. Our food is all about caring and hospitality – bringing people closer together and making people feel happy. Behind each dish, there is a story to share.

Globalization and multiculturalism are doing much to promote West African food and culture in the UK. However, there aren't many high-profile figures who champion West African food in this country, so I want to share my culture and inspire other British Africans to tell their stories through food. I think representation matters, so if someone can see a little bit of themselves in me, I hope they're encouraged to pursue their own ideas and express themselves through what they cook as I have done. More than ever before, African foods are readily available in supermarkets and online. Despite this, they're not bought as much as they might be because there's little understanding of how to use these ingredients. I've witnessed people trying West African food and I've seen the intrigue it sparks on their taste buds – they want to know about the flavours and how to make it. There are a growing number of cafés and restaurants serving West African food, but recreating these dishes at home is still out of reach for many.

Hibiscus is my first cookbook and I hope to show you a glimpse of what West African-inspired food has to offer. From over 200 of the ethnic groups in Nigeria, I've primarily focused on the cuisine of three: Yoruba, Igbo and Hausa. My aim is to create fresh, flavourful meals for every occasion. There are ingredients that you may never have come across (although I'll always try to provide an alternative where possible) and new cooking methods and techniques to try, too. You'll also find British classics with a Nigerian twist and rejuvenated recipes for everyday staples that make use of underappreciated flavour combinations. I hope these recipes can transform your cooking into something spectacular, the way they have mine.

MY STORE CUPBOARD

It's much easier to find ingredients that are used in Nigeria in Western supermarkets nowadays, especially if you live in a city. I must confess that I am a big online food shopper – a habit (or skill, in my opinion!) I picked up at university. So, if you struggle to find anything that features in the book, do have a browse online. Many of the ingredients used in Nigerian cuisine can also be found in health-food stores, as they're considered superfoods here.

In *Hibiscus*, you'll find a few exotic ingredients that you may never before have associated with Nigeria. I'm hoping (and happy!) to introduce you to some new ingredients, too. I love to experiment with novel flavours and find it incredibly rewarding, particularly when I serve something and an inquisitive look comes across everyone's face – tasting something they've never experienced, something they can't quite put their finger on. Below are my go-to ingredients and I've provided a description of the slightly more unusual ones.

FRESH INGREDIENTS

1.	YAMS	5.	GINGER	9.	LONG RED CHILLI	13.	AVOCADO
2.	CASSAVA	6.	MANGO	10.	GARLIC	14.	OKRA
3.	SWEET POTATO	7.	PEPPERS	11.	SCOTCH BONNET CHILLI	15.	GARDEN EGGS
4.	SHALLOT	8.	TURMERIC	12.	LIME	16.	PLANTAINS

YAMS are tubers with an inedible dark brown bark and a white flesh that should be completely soft before being eaten. When cooked, yams are very similar in texture to Maris Piper potatoes, but with more natural sweetness. Typically, they're eaten boiled but you can cook yams just as you would cook potatoes. They're also dried out in the sun and processed to make a flour (labelled elubo isu in African grocery stores), which can be used for Okele (see page 28) or to make dumplings (Beef and Amala Stew Pot – see page 139) and muffins (Amala Chocolate Muffins – see page 168).

CASSAVA is a large tuber with brown bark and hard, white flesh. When cooked, it has a somewhat tangy, sourdough-like taste. Like most tubers, it can be eaten boiled, steamed, roasted or fried. It's also milled into a flour that is typically used for making Okele (see page 28), or processed to make garri.

SCOTCH BONNET CHILLI is an essential aromatic used in Nigeria, where many people like their food extremely spicy. It's fine, however, to use regular long chillies if you're not keen on extra-spicy food.

OKRA, also called lady fingers, are green pods with white seeds, generally no bigger than the size of a finger. They can be eaten raw and turn slimy when overcooked. Quite plain in taste, okra are great at absorbing flavours from herbs, spices and other vegetables.

GARDEN EGGS are not to be confused with eggplants (the American name for aubergines), although they belong to the same family and are similar in texture, albeit slightly softer. They're round and white in colour (hence the name), and are best eaten cooked. I enjoy them roasted and eaten with other vegetables, such as in my Nigerian Roasted Veg (see page 35).

PLANTAINS look similar to bananas (they are a member of the same family), but are much larger and also have squarer ends. They're also less sweet, which makes them incredibly versatile, and they can be used in sweet and savoury dishes.

1.

2.

3.

5.

4.

9.

6.

7.

8.

10.

11.

12.

13.

14.

15.

16.

17.

18.

19.

20.

21.

22.

23.

24.

25.

HERBS AND SPICES

1. CAYENNE PEPPER
2. EFIRIN
3. EGUSI SEEDS
4. **DRIED BIRDSEYE CHILLIES**
5. **DRIED OREGANO**
6. **CLOVES**
7. **COCONUT FLAKES**
8. HIBISCUS

9. PAPRIKA
10. BAOBAB
11. **PEPPERCORNS**
12. **NUTMEG**
13. **DRIED BAY LEAVES**
14. **CUMIN SEEDS**
15. **CASSAVA FLOUR**
16. **CHILLI FLAKES**
17. **FINE-CUT DRIED**

    HIBISCUS
18. **DRIED THYME**
19. **CINNAMON**
20. **GARLIC GRANULES**
21. UDA
22. **GARLIC**
23. **GROUND GINGER**
24. **GROUND TURMERIC**
25. **CELERY SALT**

CAROB
MORINGA
PALM JUICE, WINE AND
    VINEGAR
RED PALM OIL
KOLA NUTS
GARRI
BEAN FLOUR
ATAMA

CAYENNE PEPPER is used a lot in Nigerian cooking – usually dried whole peppers rather than its powdered form. Nigerian dishes are more likely to be seasoned with cayenne pepper than black pepper because of Nigerian fondness for spice.

EFIRIN, also known as clove basil, is a herb with waxy, jagged leaves. It is primarily used to flavour soups in Nigeria, although it's so versatile that I use it in all sorts of dishes. Common basil is a good substitute.

EGUSI SEEDS are found inside gourds such as pumpkins and melons. They're like very flat blanched almonds in appearance, and emit a nutty aroma when toasted. Generally, they're ground and used to thicken soups and stews.

HIBISCUS is a purplish-red flower with a zesty cranberry flavour. The petals are often dried, so it can be enjoyed all year round. It's an incredibly versatile ingredient and can be used in savoury dishes with meats and in sweet recipes, too.

BAOBAB trees produce pods, in which you will find the fruit – cubes that look like fluffy, white marshmallows. In Nigeria, the fruit is snacked on because of its refreshing taste. For export, it's generally dried and processed to a nutrient-packed powder that can be found in health stores. The leaves of the baobab tree are also used for adding flavour to soups and stews.

UDA, also called Selim pepper, is native to West Africa and is often used in stews and soups. It looks like a vanilla pod, only with a thicker exterior, and the berries inside are chestnut brown with a fragrant, lemony-wood scent. They're used in the marinade for a popular Nigerian street food, suya.

CAROB, or locust bean, is a tropical pod containing a sweet pulp that is dried and ground to a chocolatey brown powder.

MORINGA is a tree widely cultivated in northern Nigeria, where its leaves are primarily eaten in soups. Its powdered form is a vivid green colour not dissimilar from matcha powder. It has a sharp taste with nutty accents.

PALM JUICE, WINE AND VINEGAR are made from palm tree sap. Upon extraction, it is a naturally sweet juice. Within a few hours, it ferments and turns to wine with a low alcohol content. Left much longer, it turns to palm vinegar.

RED PALM OIL has a unique sweet flavour with mild hints of carrot and is a similar consistency to coconut oil. In West Africa it is harvested sustainably and used in its raw form. Try to find brands that responsibly source their palm oil. If you can't find palm oil, you can cook with any other oil but the flavour and colour won't be the same – I've pointed out when really only palm oil will do!

KOLA NUTS are the main flavouring in a certain popular soft drink. The reddish-brown nut is high in caffeine and generally tastes bitter, so is often mixed with sugar. In Igbo culture, they are usually eaten whole and offered as a sign of hospitality.

GARRI is cassava that has been completely dried in the sun and shredded down to breadcrumb size. It is used to make Eba (see page 29) or is soaked in water and eaten like breakfast cereal with a sprinkling of sugar.

BEAN FLOUR is most commonly made from brown honey beans in Nigeria. They're de-hulled, dried and milled, and the resulting off-white flour is typically used to make Moin Moin (see page 65), a steamed bean cake, and Akara, bean fritters (see page 63).

ATAMA is a herb with a liquorice-like scent, very similar to tarragon, which can be used as a substitute, although its leaves are much wider – more like those of the bay tree. It can be used dried or fresh, but the former has a much more intense flavour.

Fruit, Vegetables and Tubers

BELL PEPPER SOUP

Obe Ata (Yoruba)

It wouldn't be right to have a Nigerian cookbook and not include Obe Ata. Obe means soup in Yoruba and ata means pepper. In Nigeria, soups are usually made by blending the ingredients first and then cooking them in oils and flavoured stock. When made this way, they develop a vibrant colour. Most are ruby red, rich gold or bright, emerald green, encapsulating Nigerian food to a T: rich in flavour and beautiful to look at. This recipe is really quite spicy, so feel free to reduce or omit the chilli according to your taste buds! Serve with some Agege Bread (see page 152) or brioche, with rice spooned on top, or with Okele (see page 28).

PREP TIME: 10 MINS
COOKING TIME: 20 MINS
SERVES: 4

2 large red peppers, chopped
4 salad tomatoes, halved
2 white onions, halved
2 celery sticks, chopped
 (optional)
4cm piece of fresh ginger,
 peeled and finely chopped
 (optional)
2 tbsp palm oil or coconut oil
1 beef, chicken or vegetable
 stock cube
1 tsp garlic granules
½ tsp ground cloves
1 tbsp carob powder
 (optional)
2 Scotch bonnet chillies,
 deseeded (if preferred) and
 finely chopped
salt, black pepper and
 cayenne pepper
groundnut oil, to serve

Using a blender or food processor, blitz the peppers, tomatoes, onions, celery and ginger (if using) with 100ml water to a relatively smooth liquid. You might need to do this in batches, depending on the size of your equipment.

Place a large saucepan over a medium heat and add the palm oil or coconut oil. Once it has melted, add the pepper mix, increase the heat to medium–high and cook for roughly 5 minutes until its colour changes from a pastel red to a dark, fiery red.

In a measuring jug, add 200ml boiling water to the stock cube, garlic granules, ground cloves and the carob powder, if using. Stir to dissolve the stock cube and then pour into the pan with the pepper mix. Add the chopped Scotch bonnets and season to taste with salt, black pepper and cayenne pepper. Stir, then place the lid on the pan and bring to the boil. Once boiling, reduce the heat back to medium–low and cook for a further 10 minutes until reduced to a rich soup. By this point any tanginess from the peppers should be gone and the soup will taste almost sweet.

Divide between four bowls and drizzle over some groundnut oil to serve.

❈ NOTES

Because this soup is eaten so often, many Nigerian households use double or triple the quantity of ingredients, blend the vegetables and then freeze them in portions. The frozen pepper paste can be added straight to the pan with the stock and spices. It's also very common to add some form of protein to turn the soup into a stew. Favourites include chicken thighs or drumsticks, firm white fish or diced beef and tripe.

EGUSI SOUP

Obe Egusi (Yoruba)

This is definitely one of the most popular soups in Nigeria, and one which you'll often find on the dinner table – a staple dish. It can be made in an abundance of ways – light and fresh or thick and creamy – using a vast array of cooking methods. Here's my go-to recipe. Egusi seeds are the white seeds you find in a pumpkin, squash or melon. Although they don't smell of much, they have a nutty flavour, not unlike almonds, and act as a brilliant thickening agent. If you can't find palm oil, you can try coconut oil or groundnut oil but the flavour of the dish won't be the same.

PREP TIME: 10 MINS
COOKING TIME: 25 MINS
SERVES: 4

200g ground egusi or ground
  almonds
1 chicken stock cube,
  crumbled
2 tbsp palm oil
1 red onion, thinly sliced
1 tbsp tomato purée
2 Scotch bonnet chillies,
  deseeded (if preferred) and
  finely chopped
1 tsp onion granules
1 tsp celery salt
½ tsp ground ginger
¼ tsp ground cloves
1 tbsp carob powder
2 tbsp coconut aminos or
  2 tsp shrimp paste
100g baby leaf spinach,
  chopped (optional)
salt

Add the ground egusi to a dry frying pan and toast for 4–5 minutes until it has darkened slightly. Pour the toasted egusi powder into a bowl, along with the stock cube and mix with 600ml water so that a runny paste is formed. Set aside.

Melt the palm oil in a large saucepan over a medium–low heat. Add the onion and tomato purée, stir and cook for 6 minutes until the onion has softened. Add the egusi mixture and stir until well combined. You should be left with a milky yellow blend. Add in the Scotch bonnets, onion granules, celery salt, ginger, cloves, carob powder and coconut aminos or shrimp paste to further develop the taste. Check if any additional salt is needed, then cook for 10 minutes until thickened and tiny lumps of the egusi seeds are visible. Towards the last 5 minutes, add the chopped spinach, if using, and let wilt.

When spinach is wilted, turn off the heat and let sit for 5 minutes before serving.

ATA SALAD

This is a really refreshing salad that's so simple to put together. I'm always surprised by how flavourful it is considering it contains just a handful of ingredients. It's the uncooked version of Bell Pepper Soup (Obe Ata – see page 17) and is best eaten on a hot day or when you don't particularly feel like slaving away at a stove. Nigerians don't generally consider salads to be main meals, so I tend to serve this as a starter if I'm having guests over. If you're looking for something a bit more filling, pair it with some flavoured rice or millet.

PREP TIME: 10 MINS
SERVES: 4 AS A STARTER

2 large red peppers, finely
   chopped
325g baby plum tomatoes,
   chopped
½ small red onion, finely
   chopped
4 celery sticks, chopped
4cm piece of fresh ginger,
   peeled and grated
groundnut oil, for drizzling
¼ tsp crushed chilli flakes,
   or more to taste
salt and black pepper

In a large bowl, mix together the peppers, tomatoes, red onion, celery and ginger. Drizzle over the groundnut oil and toss gently to coat everything evenly. Add the chilli flakes and season to taste.

Divide the salad onto plates and serve.

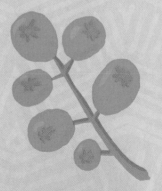

OKRA AND MANGO SALAD

At my boarding school in Nigeria, at the weekend we would go to the local swimming pool or track for sports before an afternoon siesta and a serving of fresh papaya or mango picked from the trees on campus. We never ate them in a fancy way – we weren't given knives to cut the fruit into cubes. Instead, we would cup them in our hands, peel the skins back with our teeth and bite into the flesh. This salad reminds me of those times and is filled with some of my favourite leaves and vegetables to be found in Nigeria, one of which is atama. Here, it's easiest to find in an African or Caribbean shop or online. However, with its distinctly liquorice flavour, tarragon makes the perfect substitute.

PREP TIME: 10 MINS
COOKING TIME: 5 MINS
SERVES: 4

2 tsp coconut oil
350g okra, chopped
1 small red onion, finely
    chopped
1 tbsp atama or tarragon,
    chopped
2 small mangoes or papayas

FOR THE DRESSING
6 tbsp coconut nectar or
    honey
2 tbsp freshly squeezed
    lemon juice
2 tsp crushed chilli flakes

First, make the dressing by whisking together the coconut nectar or honey, lemon juice and chilli flakes in a small bowl.

In a frying pan, heat the coconut oil over a medium–high heat until it melts and fry the okra for roughly 3 minutes. The okra should still have a slight crunch to it – if heated for too long, it will become soggy. Add the dressing, making sure the okra is evenly coated before setting aside to cool.

Put the onion and atama or tarragon leaves in a large bowl and toss thoroughly.

If using mango, remove the skin using a y-peeler, then cut the cheeks off, making sure to avoid the stone. Trim any extra flesh off the stone, then cut all the flesh into slices. If using papaya, cut it in half lengthways and deseed, then scoop out the flesh in chunks.

When you're ready to serve, evenly distribute the onion mix between four plates and top with the fruit and okra. Drizzle the juices from frying the okra on top of the salad and dig in.

FROZEN WATERMELON AND CUCUMBER SALAD

Of course, most of the time it was hot in Nigeria, but on those really sweltering days, my grandma would buy watermelons and cucumbers to be chopped and frozen. It's very rarely hot enough to warrant doing this in the UK, but on the occasions that I do make this salad, I'm instantly reminded of how deliciously refreshing these frozen treats were. A melon baller comes in handy for the recipe, but isn't essential.

**PREP TIME: 15 MINS
  PLUS FREEZING TIME
COOKING TIME: 10 MINS
SERVES: 4**

1 small watermelon
2 cucumbers
50g egusi seeds
4cm piece of fresh ginger,
  peeled and grated

FOR THE GINGER DRESSING
3 tbsp groundnut oil
1 tbsp freshly squeezed
  lemon juice
1 tbsp coconut nectar or
  honey
2 tbsp rice milk
1 tsp ground ginger
½ tsp crushed chilli flakes

Cut the watermelon in half and remove the seeds. If you have one, use a melon baller to scoop out balls. If not, cut the melon in half once more and make several cuts along each quarter being careful not to go through the bark. Use a spoon to carve out the slices then, with a knife, cut them into smaller chunks and set aside. To prep the cucumbers, peel the skin off each and halve lengthways. Scoop out the seedy bits and chop both boats into thin slices.

Put the watermelon balls and cucumber slices on to two small baking trays and spread out so that none of the pieces are touching. Carefully wrap the trays in cling film and place in the freezer for 2–3 hours. If you'd prefer not to freeze them, simply put the trays in the fridge to chill for at least an hour and take out when the dressing is ready.

While you wait, make the dressing by whisking together the groundnut oil, lemon juice, coconut nectar or honey, rice milk, ground ginger and chilli flakes in a small bowl and set aside.

Lightly toast the egusi seeds in a small frying pan over a low heat for about 5 minutes, or until they turn golden and start to pop. Transfer to a small serving dish and set aside.

Once the watermelon and cucumber are frozen solid they will look like a sea of red and green crystals. Take out of the freezer, put them in a large bowl and toss through the grated ginger.

Share the salad evenly between four bowls and serve with the dressing and egusi seeds on the side. Allow everyone to drizzle over as much dressing as they desire and sprinkle over the egusi seeds.

FENNEL AND MANGO SLAW

Fennel isn't often used in Nigerian cooking, but I've included it in this slaw because I like how its texture contrasts with the mango. The dressing is made from egusi, which is more typically used in soups to add flavour and as a thickening agent, such as Egusi Soup (Obe Egusi – see page 18). You can make the dressing with green pumpkin seeds or ground almonds instead but the flavour will be slightly different, albeit equally as tasty.

PREP TIME: 15 MINS
COOKING TIME: 5 MINS
SERVES: 4

2 fennel bulbs
2 mangoes, peeled, pitted
and chopped

FOR THE GRAPEFRUIT
EGUSI DRESSING
juice of ½ red grapefruit
4 tbsp coconut nectar or
honey
1 shallot, finely chopped
1 tbsp ground egusi seeds or
ground almonds
½ tsp salt
4 tbsp groundnut oil

First, make the dressing. In a small mixing bowl, combine all the ingredients, whisk together well and set aside.

Fill a large saucepan with water and bring to the boil. Cut the stalks off the fennel bulbs and discard them. Halve the fennel bulbs and cut out their cores. Finely slice, then cook in the boiling water for 3 minutes. Drain the fennel in a colander and rinse with cold water. Add the fennel and chopped mangoes to a large bowl and toss to combine.

To serve, pour the dressing over the fennel and mango, and toss until evenly coated. Plate the salad and enjoy.

HASSELBACK PLANTAINS WITH MUSHROOM STEAK

Ogede Inakuna (Yoruba)

Plantains were such a regular fixture in our kitchen when I was younger that they almost became part of the decor. We had them every other day – I couldn't get enough. My mum would top and tail them, score their skins and peel off their jackets before frying them as slivers in oil. This is how I liked them – the perfect marriage of fluffy potato and sweet banana. When I first started cooking plantain myself, I'd stand, spatula in one hand and lid in the other, like a Roman soldier fighting a hissing battle in the frying pan. I'd always add too much oil and use overripe plantains but I soon learnt my lesson. Since then, I've experimented lots with this versatile ingredient and this recipe plays with a new way of eating plantains – cut hasselback-style and baked.

PREP TIME: 15 MINS
COOKING TIME: 35 MINS
SERVES: 4

**FOR THE HASSELBACK
   PLANTAINS**
2 tbsp coconut oil, melted
4 yellow plantains, peeled
   and halved widthways
1 tbsp garri
4 tsp onion granules
2 tsp dried thyme
salt and black pepper
blanched kale, to serve

FOR THE MUSHROOM STEAK
1 tbsp palm wine vinegar or
   white wine vinegar
4 tbsp groundnut oil
½ tsp garlic powder
½ tsp ground ginger
½ tsp paprika
1 tsp roasted peanut flour
seeds from 2 uda pods,
   (optional)
4 portobello mushrooms

Preheat the oven to 180°C/Gas 4. Add the coconut oil to a roasting tray and place in the oven to heat up.

Slice a thin strip lengthways off each of the plantain halves; this flat base helps to ensure that they don't roll around while baking. Make a series of evenly spaced cuts, a couple of millimetres apart, along the length of the plantain, stopping roughly halfway down so that the slices remain attached at the bottom.

Transfer the plantains to the heated roasting tray, flat side down. Brush all over with the coconut oil and sprinkle with the garri, onion granules, thyme, salt and pepper. Place in the preheated oven to bake for 30 minutes, checking every so often to make sure they aren't burning. If the plantains are browning too quickly, cover them loosely with foil. Once they are golden and cooked through, remove them from the oven.

Place a frying pan over a medium heat. Working quickly, whisk together the vinegar, groundnut oil, garlic powder, ginger, paprika, peanut flour and the seeds of the uda pods, if using, in a small bowl. Brush the top and bottom of the mushrooms with the marinade and fry for 2–3 minutes on each side until softened, before placing on the plates with the plantain. Drizzle over any leftover marinade and serve hot with blanched kale.

OKELE

Okeles are the preferred dish of most Nigerians and in some sense can be seen as the West African answer to pasta. The English translation of okele is 'swallow', because it doesn't need to be chewed – rather, you let it melt in your mouth and then gulp it down.

The beginning stages of making an okele are similar to that of preparing choux pastry, but okele requires additional steaming. The process of repeatedly steaming and beating the okele does two things. Firstly, it ensures it is cooked through and develops the flavour of the okele, so that it doesn't taste like you're eating a flour paste. Secondly, it develops the starch that makes okele characteristically stretchy and sticky – without the constant beating and steaming, that starch doesn't become active.

The most common ingredients used to make okele are rice, yams, cassava or plantain, and there are two varieties: Fufu (the most popular) and Amala, which differ primarily according to how their base ingredients are prepared. Fufu usually range from pure white to off-white and their consistency varies depending on how much liquid is used – generally, for soft Fufu, there should be four times as much liquid to flour. Amala range in colour from mustard yellow to grey-brown.

On its own, an okele can be pretty bland; for that reason, Nigerians take great pride in pairing it with a combination of soups to really bring it alive. The traditional way to eat an okele is by scooping some of it by the fingers, rolling it into a ball and then coating it in the desired soup. Okele can be quite heavy so is best eaten at lunchtime, rather than for dinner.

Here are two of my go-to recipes. Eba is the easiest and fastest okele to make. It's a common weekday meal in Nigeria and great if you're trying to eat well on a budget or are craving something tummy-hugging and heart-warming. It's made from dried cassava (garri) which tastes like sourdough and contains coarse granules, making eba slightly less smooth in texture than most okele. The use of dried cassava technically makes eba an amala, but it's closer to Fufu in colour, so I like to consider it a hybrid between the two! It's best paired with Bell Pepper Soup (Obe Ata – see page 17) and Seafood Okra Soup (Obe Ila – see page 76) as seen in the photograph overleaf.

Amala Isu, or yam amala, is my grandma's favourite okele and it apparently tends to be eaten by the older generations in Nigeria. She believes it's an acquired taste and that you'll know you're matured when you start to enjoy it. She would probably shudder at my method, but this version of amala is beginner friendly. I suggest trying it alongside my Spinach and Lamb Stew (Efo Riro – see page 137) and Egusi Soup (Obe Egusi – see page 18), or as is done traditionally, with Bean Soup (Obe Gbegiri – see page 44).

EBA

PREP TIME: 5 MINS
COOKING TIME: 15 MINS
SERVES: 4

2 tbsp coconut oil (optional)
200g garri

Prepare any soups beforehand, following the recipes on the pages indicated. Fill and boil a kettle.

Add 400ml boiling water to a large saucepan and leave on a medium–high heat. If using, add the coconut oil to the pot. Once the coconut oil has completely melted, quickly pour the garri into the pan and stir well.

As the garri granules begin to absorb the water, turn the stove down to a low heat, tilt the pot towards you and, using a wooden spoon, beat the mixture until it starts to thicken and has turned translucent. Add another 400ml boiling water to the pot, cover with a lid and let steam for 3–4 minutes. Beat the eba once more until there are no visible lumps. The eba should be soft and sticky, but when pressed down holds its shape.

Divide the eba into four and wrap each portion in cling film. Let cool for a few minutes before taking out of the cling film and shaping into balls using wet hands. Serve with hot bowls of soup.

AMALA ISU

PREP TIME: 10 MINS
COOKING TIME: 40 MINS
SERVES: 4

400g dried yam flour, sifted
2 tbsp coconut oil (optional)

Prepare any soups beforehand, following the recipes on the pages indicated. Fill and boil a kettle of water.

Mix 200g of the dried yam flour with 600ml cold water until the consistency of cake batter.

If using, melt half the coconut oil in a large saucepan over a medium–high heat. Pour the amala batter into the saucepan and stir constantly for 10 minutes until the batter thickens to a wet dough. Create dents in the amala and pour in 200ml boiling water, making sure to fill every crevice. Cover and let steam for 5 minutes. Take the lid off and, using a wooden spoon, beat the amala for 3 minutes until smooth and the dough has turned mink-brown. Divide the amala into two and wrap each portion in cling film. Repeat for the remaining 200g of dried yam flour.

Take the amala out of the cling film and shape each portion into a ball using wet hands. Serve with a hot bowl of bean soup.

PLANTAIN MASH WITH GINGER CORN AND OKRA GRAVY

When I want something similar to Okele (see previous page) but don't want to spend quite as much time making it, I turn to mash. Plantain mash is sweet, light and velvety. In this recipe, I've paired it with corn seasoned with ginger, and gravy made from okra. Cumin features heavily in the flavouring of this dish – it's used lots in African and Caribbean cooking, often as part of curry powder blends. I love how its earthy taste blends with the sweet, mellowness of the plantain. Serve on its own or with Mum's Grilled Chicken Drumsticks (see page 112).

PREP TIME: 15 MINS
COOKING TIME: 25 MINS
SERVES: 4

3 yellow plantains, peeled
   and halved
100ml rice milk
2 tbsp coconut oil
1 tsp onion granules
1 tsp garlic granules
1 tsp turmeric
1 tsp ground cumin
¼ tsp cayenne pepper
grains of paradise, to serve
   (optional)

FOR THE GRAVY
1 tbsp coconut oil
8 okra fingers, wiped and
   finely chopped
3 mushrooms, finely chopped
1 tbsp plain flour
250ml vegetable stock
salt and black pepper

FOR THE CORN
4 corn cobbettes or 2 halved
   corn cobs
1 tbsp coconut oil, melted
2 tsp ground ginger
1 tsp ground nutmeg

For the gravy, melt the coconut oil in a saucepan over a medium heat. Stir in the okra along with the mushrooms and cook for 5 minutes. Add the flour and coat the vegetables before slowly pouring in the vegetable stock, whisking vigorously to combine well. Reduce the heat to medium–low and cook for 10 minutes until the gravy has thickened. Season to taste with salt and pepper.

Meanwhile, bring a large pan of water to the boil and use tongs to drop in the corn. Reduce the heat to low and simmer for 8 minutes. In a large bowl, mix the coconut oil with the ginger, nutmeg, and some salt and pepper. When the corn is ready, take it out of the pan using tongs and toss with the ginger oil mix.

Bring a large pan of salted water to the boil and add the plantains. After 10 minutes, or when the plantains turn bright yellow and can easily be pierced with a fork, drain them and mash them in the pan with the back of a fork or a potato masher until they're smooth. Return the pan to the heat and add the rice milk, coconut oil, onion granules, garlic granules, turmeric, cumin and cayenne pepper. Mix until well combined.

Distribute the mash and corn evenly on to plates, drizzle with the okra and mushroom gravy and sprinkle with a few grains of paradise, if using. Serve immediately.

AMALA CRACKERS WITH ONIONS GALORE

I like using dried yam flour for creating crackers and dumplings as well as amala (see page 28) although it can have a bitter aftertaste so it's important to season well with a contrasting flavour. The flour changes from off-white to mink-brown when mixed with a liquid, which makes a great colour for crackers. These are slightly more effort than their store-bought alternatives, but they're totally worth it. Although simple, they're very moreish, and the onion topping is the perfect accompaniment.

**PREP TIME: 25 MINS
PLUS COOLING TIME
COOKING TIME: 25 MINS
MAKES: 12–16**

200g dried yam flour
1 tsp onion granules
½ tsp dried thyme
½ tsp salt
1 tbsp coconut oil, melted
1 large egg
coarse sea salt, for sprinkling

FOR THE ONION TOPPING
2 tbsp groundnut oil
1 white onion, finely sliced
1 red onion, finely sliced
1 shallot, finely chopped
2 garlic cloves, finely
   chopped
1 tsp ground ginger
1 tsp turmeric
2 tsp carob powder
1 Scotch bonnet chilli,
   deseeded (if preferred) and
   chopped

Preheat the oven to 180°C/Gas 4.

In a large bowl, combine the yam flour, onion granules, thyme and salt. In a small bowl, whisk together the melted coconut oil, egg and 1 tsp water. Stir the egg mix into the yam flour until well combined and then, using your hands, bring the mixture together to form a slightly wet, sticky dough.

Cut two large sheets of baking paper and sandwich the dough between them. Using a rolling pin, roll out the dough to 2mm thick. Carefully remove the top layer of paper and cut the dough into rectangles measuring about 8 x 5cm. Discard the scrap edges and sprinkle the crackers with some coarse sea salt.

Transfer the entire baking paper sheet to a baking tray and bake in the preheated oven for about 12 minutes until crisp. Take the crackers out of the oven and leave to cool for 30 minutes.

While the crackers are baking, heat the groundnut oil in a frying pan over a medium heat. Add the onions, shallot and garlic and fry for 10 minutes until they are soft before adding the ginger, turmeric and carob powder. Add the Scotch bonnet to the pan, stir, and cook for a final minute before removing from the heat. Cover with a lid to keep warm.

Once the crackers are cooled, separate each rectangle and spread with the onion topping to serve.

NIGERIAN ROASTED VEG

My mum's Sunday roast dinners were the dishes that I ate most fervently. Once in a while, she would switch it up by adding the vegetables you'd expect to see from a Nigerian meal. My favourite parts were always the potatoes because of how much their crisp exterior contrasted with the fluffy interior. I didn't think I could eat anything fluffier until the day she swapped the potatoes for yams. Occasionally at university, when I had the energy to make the trek to the African food shop at the far end of town, I would gather the vegetables that weren't so easy to find in supermarkets – or were available there at a much lower price – and make this dish. Sundays were the quiet days when it was easy to remember everything you missed, but preparing this made me feel connected to home.

PREP TIME: 20 MINS
COOKING TIME: 50 MINS
SERVES: 4

¼ large puna yam, peeled and chopped
2 red onions, quartered
4 tbsp coconut oil, melted
4 salad tomatoes, quartered
16 okra fingers, halved lengthways
3 garden eggs (page 10) or 1 small aubergine, sliced into 1cm thick slices
1 yellow plantain, peeled and sliced diagonally
1 red pepper, deseeded and chopped
1 green pepper, deseeded and chopped
2 tsp thyme leaves
salt and cayenne pepper
Bell Pepper Soup (Obe Ata – page 17), to serve

Preheat the oven to 200°C/Gas 6. Fill a large saucepan with water and when boiling, add the chopped yam. Simmer for 5 minutes and then drain.

In a mixing bowl, drizzle the yam and onions with 2 tablespoons of the coconut oil and sprinkle with salt and cayenne pepper to taste. Place the yam and onion flat on a baking tray then cover with foil and place the tray just below the middle shelf in the oven. Roast for 25 minutes until the yams are knife tender.

Meanwhile, in the same bowl as before, toss the tomatoes, okra, garden eggs or aubergine, plantain and peppers, together with the remaining coconut oil, the thyme and some salt and cayenne pepper. Once the vegetables are well coated, spread them out on a baking tray, making sure they don't overlap.

When the yams and onions have had 25 minutes, remove the foil and return to the oven to cook for a further 20–25 minutes until nicely browned and crisping around the edges. At the same time, put the tray with the tomato mixture on the shelf just above the middle of the oven. Let this set of vegetables roast for 10–12 minutes before turning with tongs and then putting them back in for a further 10–12 minutes until they start to shrivel and soften.

Serve the roasted veg warm with Bell Pepper Soup (Obe Ata).

SWEET POTATO MEDLEY WITH A TARRAGON DRESSING

In Nigeria, white-flesh sweet potatoes are eaten much more commonly than their orange-flesh counterparts. Usually, they're boiled and served with eggs or they're added to soups to give them more body. In the UK, they can be found in supermarkets as well as African or Asian stores. I love their fluffy, melt-in-the-mouth texture and didn't realize how perfectly they are accompanied by tarragon until I tried this dressing.

PREP TIME: 15 MINS
COOKING TIME: 30 MINS
SERVES: 4

groundnut oil, for roasting
8 small white-flesh sweet
   potatoes, peeled and
   chopped
2 large orange-flesh sweet
   potatoes, peeled and
   chopped
4 tsp ground cloves
4 tsp onion granules
salt and white pepper (or
   black if you don't have
   white)
a squeeze of lemon juice, to
   serve

FOR THE DRESSING
80ml coconut cream
1½ tbsp palm wine vinegar or
   white wine vinegar
2 tbsp groundnut oil
2 tsp ground nutmeg
½ red onion, finely chopped
1 tbsp finely chopped
   tarragon

Preheat the oven to 180°C/Gas 4. Fill a large casserole dish 2cm deep with groundnut oil and put in the oven to warm up.

Over a high heat, bring a large pan of salted water to the boil. Once the water is boiling, add the sweet potatoes and cook for 7 minutes or until they can just about be pierced by a fork.

While the potatoes are boiling, mix together the ground cloves, onion granules, salt and white pepper in a small bowl.

When the potatoes are ready, drain them in a colander and season with the clove and onion mix. Carefully remove the casserole dish from the oven and fill with the sweet potatoes. Roast the potatoes for 10 minutes before taking them out and turning them, then return to the oven for a further 10 minutes. At this point, the potatoes will be slightly golden.

Just before the potatoes are done, make the dressing by whisking together the coconut cream, vinegar, groundnut oil and nutmeg in a bowl. Add the chopped onion and tarragon, then mix everything together.

Serve the sweet potatoes with the dressing and a squeeze of lemon juice.

UNCLE YOMI'S BAKED EGGS WITH YAM

I've never witnessed anyone cook eggs as delicately as my uncle does. Using a wooden spoon, he gently sweeps the eggs from one side of the pan to the other, almost like a slow dance in the pan. It's a family favourite, and we often sit down to eat the eggs with yams boiled in sugared water. But due to their popularity, my uncle was finding he had to make his special eggs more than once (in fact at least twice more), so we've since adopted a new method whereby the other batches cook in the oven along with the yams, so he can eat his food without it getting cold.

PREP TIME: 20 MINS
COOKING TIME: 50 MINS
SERVES: 4

½ puna yam
2 tbsp groundnut oil, plus
    extra for brushing
½ red onion, thinly sliced
2 salad tomatoes, halved and
    thinly sliced
1 Scotch bonnet chilli,
    deseeded (if preferred) and
    thinly sliced
8 eggs
1 tsp celery salt
1 tsp onion granules
1 tsp cayenne pepper
½ tsp ground cloves
salt and finely ground black
    pepper

Preheat the oven to 200°C/Gas 6.

Roughly slice the yam into six thick discs so that it's easier to handle. Using a paring knife, peel away the bark from the yam and cut each disc in half. Thinly slice each disc in half lengthways to create 'petals' – it's worthwhile using a mandolin slicer to get the petals as thin as possible. Rinse the yams in a bowl of cold water and dry on some kitchen paper.

Add 1 tablespoon of the groundnut oil to a 23cm cast-iron skillet, and make sure the entire base is well coated. Fan out the yam petals, so that they overlap each other, to form a flower that completely covers the base of the skillet. Use the remaining yam slices to create more layers. You should have roughly five layers, depending on the thickness of the yam petals. Brush the exposed yams on the top layer with groundnut oil. Bake for 20 minutes until the yams start to soften and the edges curl up.

Meanwhile, add the remaining tablespoon of oil to a frying pan, along with the onion, tomatoes and Scotch bonnet. Fry over a medium–low heat for 8 minutes until the onions have softened. Take off the heat and let cool.

Whisk the eggs in a large bowl, then add the celery salt, onion granules, cayenne pepper and ground cloves, along with the cooled, cooked vegetables. Stir until well incorporated, then carefully pour the egg mixture over the yam base. Return to the oven for a final 30 minutes until the eggs are cooked and the top is golden. Serve hot.

YAM POTTAGE

Asaro (Yoruba)

In Nigeria, my grandma would sometimes make pottage for me and my cousins. It's a really comforting dish and traditionally leans more towards porridge than soup. She always aims to please, so she would spend lots of time adjusting the spices until they were perfect. Sometimes she'd add smoked turkey or mackerel to intensify the flavour, although I haven't included any in this more conventional version. Some people like to use water yams, coco yams or plantain, but I've chosen puna yams for this recipe as they are quite floury and give a fluffy, cloud-like texture. Serve on its own sprinkled with a few chives or with Bell Pepper Soup (Obe Ata – see page 17). Alternatively, enjoy with Malt Braised Beef (see page 141) or Baobab Lamb Cutlets (see page 138). If you can't find palm oil, you can try coconut oil or groundnut oil but the flavour of the dish won't be the same.

PREP TIME: 20 MINS
COOKING TIME: 35 MINS
SERVES: 4

4 tbsp palm oil
1 small onion, chopped
1 Scotch bonnet chilli, deseeded (if preferred) and chopped
2 celery sticks, chopped
1 yellow pepper, deseeded and finely chopped
½ large puna yam, peeled and cut into chunks
1 vegetable stock cube, crumbled
1 tbsp carob powder
2 tsp onion granules
1 tsp ground ginger
½ tsp ground cloves
½ tsp ground nutmeg
1 tsp celery salt
2 tsp dried basil
salt and cayenne pepper
chives, to serve (optional)

Add the palm oil to a large saucepan over a medium–low heat and let it melt. Stir in the onion, Scotch bonnet, celery and yellow pepper. Cook for 7–10 minutes, stirring often, until the onion and pepper are softened. Using a hand-held blender, purée the vegetables until smooth.

Meanwhile, bring a large pan of salted water to a boil and carefully add in the cubed yams. Let cook, covered, for 10 minutes, until beginning to soften. Use a colander to drain the yam, reserving 250ml of the cooking water. Add the yam, along with the water, to the pan of blended vegetables, then stir in the stock cube, carob powder, onion granules, ginger, cloves, nutmeg, celery salt and basil. Cover the pan with a lid, turn the heat up to medium and cook the yams for a further 10 minutes until a fork can easily pierce through.

Once the yams are quite soft, use the back of a fork to break them apart, then mix until whipped and fluffy. Make any final taste adjustments with salt and cayenne pepper. Turn the heat down to low and let cook for a final 3 minutes, ensuring all the liquid has been absorbed by the yams.

Serve sprinkled with a few chives, if using. I find it best to let the pottage cool slightly before eating.

Grains and Pulses

CORN SOUP

Omi Ukpoka (Edo)

In this book, I wanted to feature a dish from one of the more minor ethnic groups in Nigeria, so my mother put me in touch with one of her friends who gave me a recipe for Edo corn soup. This is my adaptation, made with a Western twist. It uses ground uziza – a glossy green herb with a spicy taste, which emits a nutty, smoky aroma when cooked.

PREP TIME: 5 MINS
COOKING TIME: 15 MINS
SERVES: 4

1 tbsp palm oil or coconut oil
½ carrot, peeled and grated
½ x 200g tin sweetcorn, drained
2 tsp ground nutmeg
1 tsp ground uziza (optional)
1 vegetable stock cube, crushed
2 uda pods, crushed
3 tbsp fine cornmeal
50g uziza leaves or baby leaf spinach, chopped
1 spring onion, chopped
salt and white pepper
2 hard-boiled eggs, halved, to serve

Fill and boil a kettle.

Heat the palm oil or coconut oil in a saucepan over a medium heat. Add the grated carrot and sweetcorn along with the nutmeg and ground uziza, if using. Stir and cook for 3 minutes.

Measure 600ml boiling water in a jug and stir in the crushed stock cube until it dissolves. Add the vegetable stock and uda pods to the pan and stir. Turn up the heat and let the stock boil for 5 minutes.

Meanwhile, in a small bowl, mix the cornmeal with 80ml cold water.

Remove the uda pods from the saucepan using a spoon and stir in the cornmeal mixture. Cook for 5 minutes, stirring continuously until the soup has thickened, then season to taste with salt and white pepper.

Add the chopped uziza leaves and once they have wilted, ladle the soup into four bowls. Scatter the chopped spring onion on top of each bowl and add half a hard-boiled egg to serve.

BEAN SOUP

Obe Gbegiri (Yoruba)

Obe Gbegiri, pronounced 'beh-gee-ri', is a yellow soup made from beans and is predominantly eaten by Yoruba people. Traditionally it's eaten alongside ewedu, a green soup, and Bell Pepper Soup (Obe Ata – see page 17), a red soup, and served with an amala dish (see page 28). Growing up, this dish wasn't a favourite for me or my cousins and was favoured by the adults of the house – it does take a little while to get used to, but when you do, the flavours are really tasty. It's also a labour of love: my grandma would soak her beans before peeling off their coats one by one, and she'd always make sure to spend time blending the soup to make it as smooth as could be. I always use palm oil – it can be replaced with another oil, but the taste won't be the same.

PREP TIME: 10 MINS
COOKING TIME: 25 MINS
SERVES: 4

2 tbsp palm oil or coconut oil
1 white onion, chopped
2 yellow peppers, deseeded and chopped
4 salad tomatoes, chopped
1 Scotch bonnet chilli, deseeded (if preferred) and chopped
150g bean flour
1 vegetable stock cube
1 tsp turmeric
1 tsp onion granules
1 tsp celery salt
salt and cayenne pepper

In a large pan over a medium heat, melt the palm oil and gently cook the onion and peppers for 10 minutes until soft. Add the tomatoes and Scotch bonnet and continue cooking for 5 minutes.

While the vegetables cook, make your bean paste by mixing the bean flour with 300ml cold water until well incorporated. Once the tomatoes have broken down, add the paste to the pan and stir in.

Measure 600ml boiling water into a large measuring jug and mix in the stock cube, turmeric, onion granules and celery salt. Pour the stock into the pan, about 100 ml at a time, stirring vigorously as the soup will start to thicken. Once you have added all the stock, turn the heat up to medium–high. Add salt and cayenne pepper to season and let cook for about 7 minutes, or until thickened to your liking.

Spoon into 4 bowls to serve. Best eaten immediately.

BLACK RICE BALLS

Tuwo Shinkafa Bak'i (Hausa)

Tuwo Shinkafa are balls made from extremely soft rice, and Bak'i is the Hausa word for black. The balls are usually made with white rice such as jasmine rice, or any other variety that is prone to getting extremely soft, however for my version I'm using black rice. That being said, if you find it hard to find a variety of black rice that gets sticky when cooked, you can substitute with jasmine rice. This is a very simple recipe and traditionally it's paired with Pumpkin Soup with Turkey (Miyan Taushe – see page 120).

PREP TIME: 5 MINS
COOKING TIME: 15 MINS
SERVES: 4

200g black rice
1 handful of fresh parsley,
    chopped
1 Scotch bonnet chilli,
    deseeded and chopped
salt

Bring 425ml water to the boil in a saucepan set over a high heat and add the black rice to the pan. Bring the heat down to low, sprinkle with salt, cover with a lid and cook for 40 minutes until all the water is absorbed and the rice is sticky.

When the rice is cooked, add the fresh parsley and Scotch bonnet to the pan. Use a wooden spoon or hand-held blender to mash the rice until only a few grains are visible. Let cool slightly, then, using wet hands, mould the rice into balls the size of walnuts, using roughly 2 tablespoons of the rice mix for each one. You should be able to make about 12 balls.

Serve warm.

JOLLOF RICE

Jollof rice actually originates from Senegal, although it's popular throughout West Africa. Every country has a distinct way of making it. One might play with the cooking method, type of grain or the colours of the tomatoes and peppers used to give it a unique twist. Nigerians in particular like to use parboiled long-grain rice to create theirs. However, the one thing that can be agreed on is that if yours is soggy or looks wet, it's considered a failure – Jollof rice should never look like a risotto. It's a dish that people feel very sensitive about and many Nigerians are convinced that theirs is the best known to man. I've provided two recipes: one steamed version (shown on the left overleaf) because it's almost impossible to burn the rice when it's cooked this way, and one cauliflower version (photographed on the right overleaf). I turn to this when I'm trying to reduce my carb intake or if I just want a slightly lighter meal.

STEAMED JOLLOF RICE

PREP TIME: 15 MINS
COOKING TIME: 50 MINS
SERVES: 4

2 tbsp coconut oil
2 tbsp tomato purée
1 Scotch bonnet chilli,
    deseeded (if preferred) and
    chopped
4cm piece of fresh ginger,
    peeled and grated
½ onion, finely chopped
325g baby plum tomatoes,
    finely chopped
1 tsp dried thyme
1 tsp cayenne pepper
1 tsp black pepper
½ tsp ground cloves
1 tsp onion granules
a pinch of salt
250g basmati rice
2 or 3 bay leaves

In a frying pan set over a medium–low heat, melt the coconut oil and add the tomato purée, Scotch bonnet, ginger and onion. Fry for 5 minutes until the onion takes on a red hue. Add the chopped tomatoes – there's no need to blend them but you can do so if you prefer – along with the herbs, spices and salt. Stir well and continue frying for a further 5 minutes until the tomatoes become deep red in colour.

Meanwhile, set up the steamer by filling a saucepan with water and bring to the boil. Place the steaming pan on top and bring down the heat to medium–low.

Remove the tomatoes from the heat and add the basmati rice. Mix until the rice is well coated, then transfer the mixture to the steaming pan. Spread out evenly and top with the bay leaves. Cover and steam for 30–40 minutes, fluffing the rice with a fork every 10 minutes to make sure it is cooking evenly, until the rice is tender and cooked.

Take the steamer off the pan, fluff the rice once more and spoon on to hot plates to serve.

JOLLOF CAULIFLOWER 'RICE'

PREP TIME: 15 MINS
COOKING TIME: 15 MINS
SERVES: 4

1 red pepper, deseeded and quartered
1 orange pepper, deseeded and quartered
1 yellow pepper, deseeded and quartered
2 sprigs of thyme
1 large garlic clove, crushed
2 tbsp coconut oil, melted

FOR THE 'RICE'
1 tbsp celery salt
1 tbsp onion granules
2 tsp cayenne pepper
2 tsp crushed chilli flakes
1 vegetable or beef stock cube, crushed
1 tsp black pepper
1 tsp white pepper
1 tbsp coconut oil, melted
¼ white onion, finely chopped
2cm piece of fresh ginger, peeled and finely chopped
½ Scotch bonnet chilli, deseeded (if preferred) and finely chopped
1 large cauliflower, coarsely grated
1 tbsp tomato purée
2 sprigs of thyme
1 bay leaf
salt

Preheat the oven to 180°C/Gas 4.

In a large mixing bowl, coat the peppers, thyme and garlic in the melted coconut oil. Line a baking tray with baking paper and place the vegetables on top, making sure the peppers are skin side down. Roast for 15 minutes or until soft and slightly charred.

Meanwhile, add the celery salt, onion granules, cayenne pepper, chilli flakes, stock cube and pepper to a large frying pan and toast for 1 minute over a medium heat. Add the coconut oil and onion. After 2 minutes of sautéing (your onion won't be soft at this stage) add in the ginger and Scotch bonnet and fry for another minute.

Throw the grated cauliflower into the frying pan and stir, coating it evenly with the spices. In a small bowl mix the tomato purée with 2–3 tablespoons water – it should flow freely. Stir this into the cauliflower rice, cover the frying pan with a lid and steam for 4 minutes over a low–medium heat.

Add in the fresh herbs and season with salt to taste. Check the rice is evenly coated with the tomato mix – it should be very red at this point – and allow it to steam for a further 2 minutes.

Serve the jollof cauliflower rice hot alongside the roasted peppers.

FRIED COCONUT RICE

In Nigeria, fried coconut rice is a dish that's saved for special occasions such as weddings or birthdays, where food is usually served buffet style. Guests line up and have to make a choice between jollof rice and fried rice before selecting any accompaniments to go with it; however, in most cases both are heaped on the plate. True Nigerian fried rice contains beef liver or prawns, but I much prefer it with mushrooms instead. Likewise, the rest of the vegetables in this recipe can be swapped for any others that you prefer. In spring, I swap the green peppers with seasonal asparagus. You could easily eat this on its own or pair with a chicken recipe such as Hibiscus Chicken (see page 114) or Kola Guinea Fowl (see page 124).

PREP TIME: 15 MINS
COOKING TIME: 30 MINS
SERVES: 4

370g long-grain rice or
  basmati rice
400ml tin coconut milk
1 tbsp groundnut oil or
  coconut oil
1 chicken stock cube
½ tsp dried thyme
2 dried bay leaves
½ red onion, finely chopped
6 closed-cup mushrooms,
  wiped and chopped
½ green pepper, finely
  chopped
½ yellow pepper, finely
  chopped
1 large carrot, finely chopped
1 tsp ground coriander
¼ tsp turmeric
1 tsp garlic powder
1 tsp ground ginger
salt and white pepper

In a large saucepan, bring the coconut milk to the boil along with the stock cube, thyme and bay leaves. Reduce the heat to medium–low and allow the coconut milk to simmer for 5 minutes until it smells slightly fragrant.

Meanwhile, rinse the rice until the water runs clear. Drain the rice in a colander, then add it to the coconut milk – it should just about be covered by the liquid. Turn the heat up to medium–high, cover with a lid and cook for about 10 minutes – you'll have to stir the rice every so often to make sure it doesn't burn on the bottom. Once most of the milk has been absorbed, you'll find that if you bite on a grain of rice it should softened but still quite al dente and taste slightly nutty. Turn off the heat and set aside for the meantime.

Take a large, deep frying pan and heat the groundnut oil or coconut oil over a medium–high heat. Add the onion, mushrooms, peppers and carrot and coat them with the ground coriander, turmeric, garlic powder and ginger. Continuously stir the veggies for 7 minutes until they start to soften. Add the partly cooked rice and season with salt and pepper before reducing the heat to medium–low. Cover the pan with a lid and steam for a further 5–10 minutes, depending on how soft you like your rice.

Divide the rice evenly between four plates or place in a large serving dish for the middle of table.

PLANTAIN, BEAN AND AVOCADO RICE SALAD

Ogede, Ewa ati Iresi Afokado (Yoruba)

Here, I've given a slight makeover to the traditional rice and beans eaten in Nigeria and added avocado to the mix, which creates a creamy dish without using coconut milk. Leftover rice works perfectly for this recipe because it retains its shape better when being mixed with the other ingredients. In general, rice isn't really eaten cold in Nigeria. In fact, Nigerians hardly eat any cold food – even finger foods are usually served warm. Despite that, I'm hoping this dish will become the exception. The plantain may win them over – I don't think I've ever met a Nigerian who doesn't like plantain.

**PREP TIME: 15 MINS
PLUS COOLING TIME
COOKING TIME: 10 MINS
SERVES: 4**

- 2 avocados, pitted and peeled
- 1 tbsp freshly squeezed lemon juice
- 1 tbsp dried thyme
- 2 tsp celery salt
- 200g brown short-grain rice, cooked and cooled (from about 130g uncooked rice)
- 2 tbsp groundnut oil or coconut oil
- 1 small white onion, finely sliced
- 1 Scotch bonnet chilli, deseeded (if preferred) and finely chopped
- 2 yellow plantains, finely chopped
- 400g tin black-eyed beans or kidney beans, drained and rinsed
- salt and cayenne pepper

In a large bowl, mash the avocados with the back of a fork until creamy. Add the lemon juice, thyme and celery salt and mix. Tip in the cooled, cooked rice and stir until well combined. Season to taste using salt and cayenne pepper, then cover with cling film and set aside.

Heat the oil in a large frying pan over a medium heat and cook the onion, Scotch bonnet and plantains for 10 minutes, stirring continuously to prevent any sticking. (If you don't have a big enough pan, you may have to split the mix between two smaller pans and stir them in turn.) Once the onion is soft and the plantains have turned golden brown, transfer to a separate bowl and let cool for roughly 5 minutes.

Add the drained beans and cooled plantain mix to the rice and avocado, toss to combine and serve.

❄ NOTES

Cooked plantain hardens when left to cool for too long and its texture changes when reheated, so it's best to eat this salad soon after cooking. If you want to make this ahead of time, I suggest tossing the rest of the salad ingredients together early and cooking the plantain 5–10 minutes before serving.

ABEOKUTA BOWL

For me, the Abeokuta bowl is a collection of all my favourite food memories from that place. Abeokuta, located north of Lagos, was where I would stay with my family during half-term breaks. For our mid-week meal, we would have stewed beans and dodo (fried plantains) because it was easy to make, and I liked my beans mushy. On weekends we would go for a family trip to get grilled corn, suya and epa (roasted peanuts) before coming back to sit in the garden and watch the sunset. Don't be put off by the long list of ingredients in this recipe – it's not as complicated as it seems. Lots of bits are made simultaneously, so if you're worried about burning anything, then I recommend setting a few timers on your phone to avoid any kitchen disasters.

PREP TIME: 15 MINS
COOKING TIME: 35 MINS
SERVES: 4

200g millet or short-grain
  brown rice
1 vegetable stock cube
1 tbsp garri, to serve
4 tbsp cashews or peanuts,
crushed, to serve

FOR THE ROASTED CORN
1 tbsp groundnut oil
2 sweetcorn cobettes or
  1 sweetcorn cob
1 tsp crushed chilli flakes

FOR THE FRIED PLANTAIN
2 tbsp coconut oil
2 yellow plantains, peeled
  and sliced

FOR THE MUSHY BEANS
400g tin pinto beans
1 tsp onion granules
¼ tsp cayenne pepper
½ tsp ground cloves

In a large saucepan, toast the millet or rice over a medium heat for 5 minutes. The millet will give off a nutty smell but be careful to make sure it doesn't burn. Measure 450ml boiling water into a jug and add the stock cube, stirring vigorously to help it dissolve. Pour the vegetable stock into the millet and turn up the heat to high. Once the millet begins to boil, bring the heat right down, cover and leave to cook for 15 minutes, stirring gently now and then. Remove the millet from the heat and let it stand for 10 minutes so that any additional liquid can be absorbed.

Meanwhile, lightly oil a baking tray and roll each corn cobbette around in the oil. Bake in the oven for 20 minutes before removing the tray from the oven and turning each cob over. Sprinkle with the chilli flakes and bake for a further 15 minutes. When the corn is golden and blistered, take it out of the oven and place on to a plate to cool for 5 minutes. Using a knife, strip off the corn kernels and discard the cob.

When the corn and millet have been cooking for half their time, prepare the fried plantains by melting the coconut oil in a frying pan over a medium–low heat. Fry the plantains for 5 minutes on each side – they should be golden brown all over.

For the mushy beans, pour the pinto beans, along with their liquid, into another small pan and add the onion granules and cayenne pepper. Add salt and pepper to taste then leave to cook for 5 minutes. Once most of the liquid has evaporated, mash the beans until you have a coarse texture.

FOR THE SUYA MUSHROOM AND ONION MIX

2 tsp roasted peanut flour
2 tsp ground ginger
1 tsp garlic granules
1 tsp onion granules
1 tsp ground nutmeg
12 closed-cup mushrooms, sliced
½ large red onion, finely chopped
1 tbsp groundnut oil
1 uda pod, crushed
salt, black pepper and cayenne pepper

While the beans are cooking, combine the peanut flour, ginger, garlic and onion granules and nutmeg, and some salt and black pepper and cayenne pepper in a bowl. Toss the mushrooms and onion in the mixture. Using the same frying pan as for the plantains, heat the groundnut oil and add the mushroom and onion mix with the crushed uda pod. Allow to cook slowly, on a medium heat, for 5 minutes, stirring frequently.

To serve, fluff the millet and divide into four bowls. Top with a few spoons of the roasted corn, the suya mushroom and onion mix, mushy beans and the plantain. Finish by sprinkling on some garri and crushed cashew nuts.

BELL PEPPERS STUFFED WITH CARROT RICE FUFU

When I'm told that something can only be done a certain way, there's a part of me that takes joy in proving people wrong. It's not to be obnoxious, it's more to encourage people to try new things and not limit their creativity. Fufu is always served alongside something and never infused with anything. Here I've stepped away from the norm by cooking ground rice in vegetable stock and adding in carrots for a subtle sweetness, while staying true to Nigerian culture with the use of palm oil, peppers, peanut butter and a range of spices.

PREP TIME: 20 MINS
COOKING TIME: 40 MINS
SERVES: 4

200ml vegetable stock
100g ground rice
2 tbsp palm oil or coconut oil
1 onion, finely chopped
1 Scotch bonnet chilli,
    deseeded (if preferred) and
    finely chopped
½ large carrot, peeled and
    finely grated
1 tbsp peanut butter or
    cashew butter
2 tsp carob powder
¼ tsp turmeric
¼ tsp ground cloves
½ tsp ground nutmeg
1 tsp ground ginger
2 yellow peppers, halved
    lengthways and deseeded
2 red peppers, halved
    lengthways and deseeded
salt and cayenne pepper
crushed peanuts or cashews,
    to serve
parsley leaves, to serve

In a large saucepan, heat the vegetable stock over a high heat. Once boiling, bring the heat down to low and quickly pour the ground rice into the pan, stirring to get rid of any lumps. Beat the ground rice until thick, add 100ml boiling water to the pan, then put the lid on and let steam for 3 minutes. Repeat this step one more time, beating the ground rice, adding 100ml water and letting it steam again, then transfer the mixture to a bowl, cover and let cool.

Melt the palm oil or coconut oil in a large frying pan over a medium heat. Add the onion, Scotch bonnet and carrot to the pan and fry for roughly 7 minutes until the onion and carrot are soft. Stir in the peanut butter or cashew butter, carob powder and spices and mix until well combined, then take off the heat. Fold the cooked vegetables into the cooled rice fufu until evenly distributed and the fufu has turned orange.

Preheat the oven to 180°C/Gas 6 and line a baking tray with baking paper. Spoon the carrot rice fufu mix into the pepper halves, overfilling slightly. Place the peppers on to the tray as you go along. Once finished, cover the entire tray loosely with foil. Bake for 15–20 minutes until the peppers are heated through and somewhat soft.

Serve each person one red and one yellow stuffed pepper, sprinkled with crushed peanuts and parsley.

HERBY MILLET WITH GREEN BEANS

Unlike most Nigerian grains, millet is very subtle and doesn't attack the taste buds. It pairs really nicely with many Nigerian herbs such as efirin, for which basil is a close match. This dish is best enjoyed in the summer months. I like to cook it for my family when we have barbecues or picnics.

**PREP TIME: 10 MINS
  PLUS COOLING TIME
COOKING TIME: 20 MINS
SERVES: 4**

200g millet
1 tbsp coconut oil
1 white onion, chopped
1 Scotch bonnet chilli,
  deseeded (if preferred) and
  chopped
1 green pepper, finely
  chopped
1 tbsp finely chopped efirin
  or basil leaves,
1 tbsp finely chopped parsley
salt and black pepper
spring onions, chopped, to
  serve

FOR THE GREEN BEANS
1 tbsp coconut oil
400g tin green beans,
  drained
1 tbsp coconut aminos or
  1 tsp shrimp paste
1 vegetable stock cube,
  crumbled
1 tsp onion granules

Bring a saucepan of 500ml salted water to the boil. Add the millet, turn the heat down to medium–low and cook for 8 minutes, or until the water has all been absorbed and the millet is tender. Put the cooked millet in a bowl and set aside.

In the same saucepan, melt the coconut oil and add the onion, Scotch bonnet and green pepper. Cook for 5 minutes over a low heat until the onion is soft. Add the millet back into the pan along with the efirin and parsley and season with salt to taste. Gently mix everything together. Cover and steam for a further 2 minutes before setting aside to cool for 10 minutes.

For the green beans, melt the coconut oil in a frying pan. Add the green beans along with the coconut aminos or shrimp paste, stock cube and onion granules and mix well. Reduce the heat and let the beans heat through for 3–4 minutes. Season with salt and pepper to taste.

To serve, fluff the millet and spoon on to plates. Share out the green beans evenly, sprinkle with the spring onions and enjoy hot.

ONION MILLET WITH ROASTED GARRI TOMATOES

Back in sixth form, healthy eating was a hot topic of conversation. I had a friend who was devastated to find out that couscous wasn't actually a grain, but coarse granules made from semolina. Having hampered her gluten-free crusade, I suggested that millet would make a great alternative, especially as she wasn't a fan of quinoa. Like couscous, millet is fluffy when cooked and, like quinoa, it contains a decent amount of protein — the best of both worlds. You can easily find millet online or in health-food stores.

PREP TIME: 10 MINS
COOKING TIME: 20 MINS
SERVES: 4

1 tbsp coconut oil
½ red onion, finely chopped
1 garlic clove, finely chopped
1 vegetable stock cube,
    crushed
200g millet
1 tsp onion granules
1 tsp garlic powder
1 tsp celery salt
salt and black pepper

FOR THE TOMATOES
groundnut oil, for drizzling
300g cherry tomatoes, halved
garri or panko breadcrumbs,
    for sprinkling

Preheat the oven to 180°C/Gas 4 and drizzle a baking tray with groundnut oil.

Season the tomatoes with salt and pepper and place them cut side up on the baking tray. Sprinkle the garri or breadcrumbs all over, making sure the tomatoes are well coated. Bake for 20 minutes until the tomatoes are lightly browned.

Meanwhile, melt the coconut oil in a large frying pan over a medium heat. Add the onion and garlic and cook for 5 minutes, stirring occasionally. Add in 500ml water and the crushed stock cube, and turn up the heat to high. Once boiling, bring the heat down to medium–low, add the millet and simmer for 10 minutes. Season with the onion granules, garlic powder and celery salt. Add salt and pepper to taste and leave to cool for 10 minutes until all the water is absorbed and the grains have puffed up into teeny yellow balls.

To serve, fluff the millet with a fork and evenly spoon the millet and tomatoes on to plates. Serve hot.

BEAN FRITTERS

Akara (Yoruba)

My favourite mornings in boarding school were the ones where we were served Akara and fermented corn custard (Ogi – see page 173) for breakfast. The outside of the fritters were always crisped to perfection, while the inside was soft and airy. Akara also works well as a light lunch or, if you manipulate the shape and size, a savoury dessert. Serve as below with Greek yoghurt or in the traditional fashion with Bell Pepper Soup (Obe Ata – see page 17) and Ogi on the side.

PREP TIME: 10 MINS
COOKING TIME: 20 MINS
SERVES: 4

1 onion, quartered
2 celery sticks, chopped
200g bean flour
1 tsp onion granules
1 tsp celery salt
1 tsp garlic granules
1 tsp white pepper
1 Scotch bonnet chilli,
    deseeded (if preferred) and
    chopped
groundnut oil, for frying
salt and cayenne pepper
Greek yoghurt, to serve

Using a food processor or blender, blitz the onion and celery with up to 60ml water – you are looking for a wet purée, but not a juice. Meanwhile, sift the bean flour and the spices into a large bowl and season with salt and cayenne pepper. Pour in the onion mix and chopped Scotch bonnet and gently fold together, making sure to scrape down the sides, until a thick, wet batter is formed.

When you're ready to cook the akara, fill a heavy-based saucepan with groundnut oil to a depth of at least 4cm and set over a medium–high heat. Once the oil is hot, carefully dot 4–6 tablespoons of the batter around the pan. After 3 minutes, flip the akara over and cook on the other side for a further 2 minutes. Press down on each akara to make sure there is no uncooked batter. Repeat in batches until all the batter has been used up. You should have 16–20 fritters, depending on how heaped your tablespoons were.

Use a slotted spoon to transfer each batch to a cooling rack and place some kitchen paper underneath to catch any excess oil. Serve the akara on small plates with some Greek yoghurt.

❀ NOTES

When you've finished cooking and the oil has cooled down, pass the oil through a sieve into a small Tupperware container to get rid of any burnt fritter remnants. Cover the 'purified' oil and use later in a different recipe, such as Puff Puff (see page 156), Ijebu Fish Rolls (see page 82) or Kuli Kuli (see page 169). If you're not a fan of deep frying, you can shallow fry the fritters in a small frying pan with 2 heaped tablespoons melted coconut oil. Just make sure to dilute the batter with 250ml water beforehand and spoon blini-sized puddles of batter into the pan instead.

MOIN MOIN

Without fail, just before I left to go back to boarding school, my grandma would always make Moin Moin. I helped her peel the beans and watched as they were ground into a batter. She would then teach me how to make cones shaped from banana leaves (I never got any good at it), while I would hold them as she poured the batter in. As the pudding steamed away, my cousins and I would play around the house and every so often I would bug my grandma by asking her whether or not the Moin Moin was ready. There isn't a direct translation for Moin Moin. As with Chin Chin, its name is probably an interpretation of the sound or feeling you get when eating it.

PREP TIME: 10–15 MINS
COOKING TIME: 1 HOUR
SERVES: 4

1 uma leaf or banana leaf
  (optional)
2 tbsp coconut aminos
  (optional)
4 tbsp coconut oil, melted
1 tbsp tomato purée
1 tsp celery salt
1 tsp onion granules
1 tsp ground nutmeg
1 onion, chopped
½ Scotch bonnet chilli,
  deseeded (if preferred)
1 large red pepper, chopped
200g bean flour
salt, white pepper and
  cayenne pepper

FOR THE SOAKED GARRI
100g garri, to serve
1–2 tbsp sugar, to serve

If using, cut out four small circles and four larger circles from the uma or banana leaf using the base and top of a pudding mould. If you don't have leaves, you can use baking paper instead. Oil four pudding moulds and place a small circle cut out in the base of each one. Set the moulds and larger leaf circles aside.

In a jug, mix 350ml water with the coconut aminos, if using, melted coconut oil, tomato purée, celery salt, onion granules and nutmeg.

In a blender or food processor, blend the onion, Scotch bonnet and red pepper with the coconut aminos and tomato mixture. Add the bean flour and blend once more until well combined and smooth. Season with salt and white and cayenne peppers. Pour the bean batter into the lined pudding moulds and top with the larger leaf circles.

Set up the steamer by filling a medium saucepan with water and bringing to the boil. Place the steaming pan on top and put the puddings inside. Turn the heat down to medium–low, cover the steamer with a lid and leave to cook for 1 hour.

To test if the moin moin is ready, lift the uma cover and pierce the centre with a skewer or knife – it should come out clean. Turn off the heat and remove the moulds from the pan. Let the puddings sit in the moulds for 30 minutes, then use a small palette knife to loosen the sides of the puddings before inverting the moulds on to plates.

While the puddings are resting, add the garri to a bowl and top with 400ml water. Add sugar to taste and then serve with the moin moin.

JAND BOWL

In Nigeria, Jand is the colloquial term for England. I've called this dish the Jand Bowl as all the ingredients are chosen because they're as easy to find in UK supermarkets as they are in Nigeria. It's a recipe that will keep you full, and not overwork you in the kitchen.

PREP TIME: 20 MINS
COOKING TIME: 30 MINS
SERVES: 4

Steamed Jollof Rice or Jollof
    Cauliflower 'Rice' (page 46)
1 large sweet potato, peeled
2 tbsp flaked almonds
200g baby leaf spinach
1 tbsp freshly squeezed
    lemon juice
400g tin black-eyed beans,
    drained
1 avocado
2 sprigs of tarragon, leaves
    picked
salt, black pepper and
cayenne pepper

FOR THE DRESSING
2 tbsp groundnut oil or
    walnut oil
1 tbsp freshly squeezed
    lemon juice
½ tsp cayenne pepper

Make the dressing by whisking together the groundnut oil, lemon juice and cayenne pepper. Season with salt and black pepper to taste and whisk once more. Set aside.

Make either the Steamed Jollof Rice or Jollof Cauliflower 'Rice' as per the instructions on page 46.

Meanwhile, use the mandolin side of a box grater to slice the sweet potato into thin circles, then rinse in a bowl of water. Bring a large pan of water to the boil, add the sweet potato slices and let cook for 15 minutes until soft. Once the sweet potatoes are ready, drain in a colander.

Take a small frying pan and place it over a medium heat. Making sure the pan is dry, toast the flaked almonds for roughly 5 minutes over a low heat until browned in some areas.

Roughly chop up the spinach and put it in a bowl with the lemon juice and some salt. In a separate bowl, mash up the beans and season with some salt and cayenne pepper. Lastly, halve the avocado and remove the stone. Make several cuts horizontally and vertically in each avocado half and turn the skin inside out so that the cubes pop out and can be easily sliced off the skin.

Dollop some of the bean mash into the centre of four shallow bowls. Spoon a quarter of the jollof rice into the side of each bowl, followed by the lemon spinach, sweet potato discs, flaked almonds and avocado to create a rainbow ring of vegetables. Sprinkle over the tarragon leaves, drizzle with the dressing and serve.

SAVOURY MILLET PORRIDGE

Hausa Koko (Hausa)

During my university exams, student life saw me relying heavily on breakfast cereals for dinner. However, when I grew tired of the sugar rushes and the savoury cravings kicked in, porridge was the saviour of the day (or should I say night?). I found I preferred using millet flakes, as opposed to oats, because I felt less lethargic and able to push through the long study sessions. The millet easily takes on flavour and is the perfect base for all the spices and vegetables used in the recipe. The spices used here are inspired by a dish called hausa koko, a porridge eaten by Hausa people in Ghana, too.

PREP TIME: 20 MINS
COOKING TIME: 25 MINS
SERVES: 4

400ml tin coconut milk
200g millet flakes
1 vegetable stock cube
1 tsp onion granules
1 tsp celery salt
1 tsp ground ginger
¼ tsp ground cloves
2 tbsp coconut oil
250g okra, sliced
2 tsp carob powder
1 tsp caster sugar
1 tsp chilli flakes
1 tbsp freshly squeezed
   lemon juice
salt and cayenne pepper
4 fried eggs, to serve

In a large pan, bring the coconut milk to the boil over a high heat. Once boiling, reduce the heat to medium and add the millet flakes along with the chicken stock. Add the onion granules, celery salt, ground ginger and ground cloves. Mix until well combined, then season with salt and cayenne pepper. Cook for 15 minutes until the flakes have completely absorbed the coconut milk.

Meanwhile, melt the coconut oil in a small frying pan over a medium heat. Toss the okra in the carob powder, sugar and chilli flakes. Cook for 3 minutes until slightly softened, then sprinkle over the lemon juice. Set aside.

Once the millet is cooked, ladle the porridge into four bowls. To serve, top each bowl with some okra and a fried egg. Enjoy hot or warm.

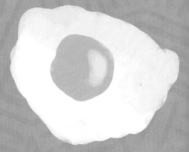

RICE CRUMPET

Sinasir (Hausa)

In the northern parts of Nigeria, there's a rice dish called Sinasir, cooked similarly to how you would make a crumpet. It's made from a mix of fermented uncooked rice, cooked rice, onions and sometimes flour. The proving time is longer than your usual crumpet, but it's worth the wait. Although it's cooked like a crumpet, it won't yield the same texture, as rice flour doesn't cook the same way. Like most Nigerian dishes, Sinasir is eaten with something savoury, and as pumpkin is popular in the northern parts I've paired the Sinasir with some fried, nutty pumpkin.

PREP TIME: 20 MINS
   PLUS FERMENTING TIME
COOKING TIME: 30 MINS
SERVES: 4

120g rice flour
160g plain flour
4 tsp onion granules
3 tsp fast-action dried yeast
4 tbsp cooked jasmine rice
4 tsp caster sugar
6 tbsp coconut yoghurt or
   Greek yoghurt
240ml rice milk, warmed
1 tsp bicarbonate of soda
½ tsp salt
coconut oil, for greasing and
   frying

FOR THE PUMPKIN
400g (prepared weight)
   pumpkin or butternut
   squash, peeled, deseeded
   and chopped
1 tbsp groundnut oil
100ml vegetable stock
1 handful of kale, finely
   chopped
3 tbsp peanut butter or
   cashew butter
salt and cayenne pepper

In a large bowl, mix the rice flour, plain flour, onion granules and yeast together. In another large bowl, using a wooden spoon, mash the cooked rice, then add the sugar and the coconut or Greek yoghurt, a tablespoon at a time. Pour the thickened rice yoghurt into the flour mix and stir to a crumbly mixture. Turn the crumbs into a batter by adding the warm rice milk, stirring until well combined. Let rest, covered, in a warm place for 30 minutes.

Whisk the bicarbonate of soda and salt into 150ml warm water and let dissolve. Beat the soda water into the rice batter for about 3 minutes until smooth looking. Cover the batter with cling film and let rest for about 4 hours or overnight.

Once the sinasir batter has fermented, lightly grease a large frying pan and 4 egg rings with coconut oil. Place the pan over a medium heat and sit the egg rings in the pan. Stir the rice batter and pour a ladleful of batter into each egg ring; the batter should come halfway up the sides. After 4 minutes, the surface of the sinasir should be covered with bubbles. Carefully remove the rings, then flip the sinasir to reveal a browned underside, and cook for a further 2 minutes. Remove from the pan and place the sinasir on a wire rack to cool while you repeat the process to cook 4 more crumpets, wiping and re-oiling the pan and egg rings first.

Alternatively, if you don't have egg rings, add half the batter to a large frying pan to form 1 large crumpet, and wait for the top to bubble. Once no more bubbles form, carefully flip the sinasir and continue to cook for a further 2 minutes. Remove the sinasir from the pan and cut into four, then repeat with the remaining batter to make 8 pieces in total, wiping and re-oiling the pan first.

While the sinasir rests, put a small pan over a medium–high heat and fry the pumpkin in the groundnut oil for 5 minutes until golden. Pour in the vegetable stock and turn the heat down to low. Cover and let cook for 10 minutes until a fork can easily pass through. Once ready, drain the pumpkin in a colander. Toss the pumpkin with the kale and peanut butter or cashew butter in a large bowl and season with some salt and cayenne pepper to taste.

When everything is ready, plate 2 crumpets per person and top with the peanut butter pumpkin. If you want, you could toast your sinasir before adding the pumpkin, otherwise serve immediately.

Fish and Seafood

CRAB AND YAM PEPPER SOUP

My first recollection of eating pepper soup was at a Nigerian restaurant my mother used to take me to when I was still in primary school. The restaurant was called Labalaba (butterfly) and was situated somewhere in Brixton. Their pepper soup was a rich broth, filled with tender goat meat. It didn't look hot, but after two or three spoonfuls my nose would be stinging from the intensity of the spice. Despite that, I would keep gulping the soup down because it was so full of other flavours. I wasn't alone in this — I once watched a man break out in a sweat and start dabbing his head profusely with a handkerchief. He would dab his forehead twice, sip the soup, pause and repeat. Pepper soup can also be made using catfish, but I enjoy mine with crab. However, there is no reason you can't add a range of different seafood. The secret ingredient that makes this dish so moreish is calabash nutmeg. As it's not easy to find, I've substituted a range of different spices close in flavour.

PREP TIME: 15 MINS
COOKING TIME: 15 MINS
SERVES: 4

4 whole cloves
1 cinnamon stick
1 whole nutmeg
4 uda pods, crushed
   (optional)
1 tsp cumin seeds
2 tbsp coconut oil
1 onion, thinly sliced
1–2 Scotch bonnet chillies,
   pierced
400g puna yam, peeled,
   washed and diced into 1cm
   cubes
2 bay leaves
2 tsp shrimp paste
1 fish stock cube
1 chicken stock cube
2 x 170g tins crab meat,
   drained or 340g fresh
   prepared crab meat
salt and cayenne pepper
efirin leaves or basil leaves,
   finely chopped, to serve

Put the cloves, cinnamon stick, nutmeg, uda pods, if using, and cumin seeds into a small dry frying pan set over a medium–high heat. Shake the pan constantly for 1–2 minutes to keep the spices from burning. Once they've darkened slightly and your kitchen smells fragrant, take the pan off the heat, cut the nutmeg in two and crush the other spices slightly. Put the spices into a bowl and set aside.

Melt the coconut oil in a large stock pot over a medium heat. Add the onion and pierced Scotch bonnets and cook for roughly 4 minutes. Stir the yam into the onion, along with the crushed spices and bay leaves. Mix the shrimp paste and stock cubes with 800ml hot water, add to the pan and turn up the heat. Once bubbling, turn the heat down to low and let cook, covered, for 10 minutes until the yam can easily be pierced with a fork. Taste and season with salt and cayenne pepper and cook for a final 2 minutes. Discard the Scotch bonnet, any large pieces of spice and the bay leaves.

To serve, evenly divide the yams between four bowls, followed by the crab meat. Ladle soup into each bowl and sprinkle with efirin or basil. Enjoy hot.

❀ **NOTES**
If you prefer your yam chopped into larger squares you'll need to increase the cooking time.

SEA BASS AND AUBERGINE SOUP

This dish is modelled after garden egg sauce – a Nigerian street food usually served with boiled yams or plantain. It's made by softening onions and carob beans in palm oil, then adding finely chopped and boiled garden eggs along with some smoked fish. As garden eggs are a bit tricky to find in the UK, I've used aubergines instead. They have a very similar flavour and the cooking process produces a silky smooth dish which is perfect for chilly autumnal days.

PREP TIME: 20 MINS
COOKING TIME: 1 HOUR
   50 MINS
SERVES: 4

3 aubergines, halved
   lengthways
1 white onion, halved
1 red pepper, halved
1 tbsp coconut oil, melted
   (plus 2 tbsp, if frying the
   fish)
1 tbsp palm oil or coconut oil
1 red Scotch bonnet chilli,
   deseeded (if preferred) and
   chopped
1 tsp carob powder
1 tbsp tomato purée
1 tbsp shrimp paste
1 tsp celery salt
1 tsp turmeric
1 tsp black pepper
4 sea bass fillets
salt and black pepper

Preheat the oven to 180°C/Gas 4.

Place the aubergines, onion and red pepper on a large baking sheet, cut side down, and brush with the coconut oil. Roast for 40 minutes–1 hour until the vegetables are soft and their skins are blistered. Remove from the oven and leave them to cool down. Peel the skins off the vegetables and discard, then purée the vegetables in a blender or food processor (you may need to do this in batches).

In a large saucepan, heat the palm oil or coconut oil and add in the vegetable purée. Add 800ml water, the Scotch bonnet, carob powder, tomato purée and shrimp paste. Bring to the boil, then turn the heat down to low. Allow the soup to cook for 40 minutes. Season with the celery salt, turmeric and black pepper. Stir and taste for any additional adjustments. Leave the soup to cook for another 5 minutes.

Meanwhile, set up the steamer by filling a saucepan with water and bringing them to the boil. Put the steaming pan on top and place the sea bass inside, skin side down. Sprinkle the fish with a little salt and some pepper, cover with a lid and let steam for 5 minutes until cooked through. Alternatively, season the fish with a little salt and pepper then heat a frying pan and add 2 tablespoons coconut oil. Once the oil is fully melted and coating the bottom of the pan, add the fillets carefully, skin side down, pressing with a spatula so that they don't curl up. Let the fillets cook for 3 minutes so the skin crisps up before flipping on to the flesh side to cook for a final 2 minutes.

To serve, pour the soup into 4 shallow bowls and lay the fish on top.
Enjoy warm.

BAOBAB AND SMOKED SALMON SOUP

Miyan Kuka (Hausa)

In the northern parts of Nigeria, it's more common to eat the leaves of the baobab tree than it is to eat the marshmallow-like fruit in their pods. This is the part of the tree you'll generally find in Europe – the white cubes are processed into a nutrient-packed powder and distributed to health-food stores. This soup is a showcase for the zesty flavour of baobab fruit.

PREP TIME: 10 MINS
COOKING TIME: 40 MINS
SERVES: 4

1 tbsp coconut oil
1 onion, chopped
2cm piece of fresh ginger, peeled and grated
2 fish or vegetable stock cubes
2 carrots, finely chopped
4 small white flesh sweet potatoes, finely chopped
2 tbsp baobab powder
200g smoked salmon, cut into strips
salt, coarsely ground black pepper and cayenne pepper

FOR THE PLANTAIN CROUTONS
1 green plantain
1 tsp onion granules
1 tsp celery salt
2 tbsp groundnut oil

Preheat the oven to 180°C/Gas 4 and line a baking tray with baking paper.

Heat the coconut oil in a large pan set over a medium heat. Add the onion along with the ginger and cook for 8 minutes until softened. Add the stock cubes and 1 litre water, increase the heat to high and bring the pan to the boil. Once boiling, reduce the heat to medium and add the carrots and sweet potatoes. Stir in the baobab powder and cook for 20 minutes until the potatoes and carrots are soft.

Meanwhile, peel the plantain by chopping off its ends and slitting its jacket lengthways to help aid its removal. Chop the plantain into little cubes and coat them in a mix of the onion granules, celery salt and groundnut oil. Spread on the lined baking tray and bake for 15 minutes until golden and crispy.

Once the soup vegetables are tender, use an immersion blender to blitz until smooth. Otherwise, blitz the soup in batches using a food processor. Add the smoked salmon into the puréed soup, stir through, then taste and season with salt and pepper.

To serve, ladle the soup into four bowls and sprinkle the plantain croutons on top. Enjoy warm.

SEAFOOD OKRA SOUP

Obe Ila Osun (Yoruba)

More than anything, my mother loves seafood paired with okra. The happier she is, the more likely she is to use the most lavish seafood. And for her, the key to making a really good okra soup is making sure that the okra is chopped as finely as possible. Serve on its own or with Eba (see page 29) and Bell Pepper Soup (Obe Ata – see page 17), as in the photograph on page 31.

PREP TIME: 15 MINS
COOKING TIME: 25 MINS
SERVES: 4

4 tbsp coconut oil
1 onion, finely chopped
1 Scotch bonnet chilli, deseeded (if preferred) and chopped
30 okra fingers, finely chopped (tops and bottoms removed)
1 vegetable stock cube, crushed
1 tsp dried dill
2 sea bass fillets, chopped
165g raw king prawns
80g squid rings, cleaned
salt and cayenne pepper

In a large pan, melt 2 tablespoons coconut oil over a medium heat. Stir in the onion and cook for 5 minutes until it starts to soften. Add the Scotch bonnet and okra, then fry for a further 2 minutes.

Season with the vegetable stock cube and dill. Add 300ml water and when the soup starts to boil, turn the heat down to low and let it simmer for 10 minutes.

Add the sea bass, prawns and squid to the soup. Cook for 4 minutes or until the sea bass and squid turn opaque and the prawns are pink and cooked through. Season with salt and cayenne pepper, stir, then remove from the heat and serve.

MACKEREL AND ABACHA SALAD

Like with most salads, Nigerians wouldn't consider this to be a main meal, although frankly, it's filling enough that it could well be. This dish is particularly popular in Igbo culture, where it's traditionally made from peeled cassava tubers that are left to soak overnight and are then dehydrated in the sun – but I'm a bit too impatient for that. I've used puna yams in mine to create yam hash browns for a bit of a twist. The mackerel fillets add a salty dimension, which makes the salad particularly moreish.

PREP TIME: 30 MINS
COOKING TIME: 30 MINS
SERVES: 4

4 garden eggs or
  2 aubergines, thickly sliced
4 tbsp groundnut oil
2 smoked mackerel fillets,
  skinned and flaked
85g baby leaf spinach,
  chopped
salt and cayenne pepper
chilli oil, to serve

FOR THE HASH BROWNS
300g puna yam
1 red onion, finely chopped
1 large egg, beaten
2 tbsp coconut aminos or
  2 tsp shrimp paste
1 tbsp carob powder
1 tsp onion granules
1 tsp celery salt
½ tsp ground cloves
½ tsp ground cinnamon
½ tsp ground nutmeg
seeds from 1 uda pod,
  crushed
½ tsp ground cumin
120ml groundnut oil or
coconut oil

Preheat the oven to 180°C/Gas 4.

To make the hash browns, cut the puna yam into large, thick discs so that it's easier to handle. Using a paring knife, peel away the bark from the yam and cut each disc in half. Grate the yam slices and place in a large bowl filled with cold water. Rinse the grated yam in the water and drain to remove any impurities. Pat dry with kitchen paper and squeeze out any excess moisture. Transfer the grated yam to a bowl and add the chopped onion, beaten egg, coconut aminos or shrimp paste, carob powder, onion granules, celery salt and spices and season with salt. Mix until well combined and set aside.

Brush the garden egg, or aubergine, slices with the groundnut oil. Sprinkle with some salt and cayenne pepper and roast in the preheated oven for 30 minutes until slightly tender and browned.

Meanwhile, in a large non-stick frying pan, melt the oil over a medium–high heat. Dot 2 tablespoons of the yam mix per hash brown into the pan and flatten with the back of the spoon – you should have enough room to cook 4 at a time. Cook for 5 minutes on each side; they should be both crisp and browned when ready. Transfer on to some kitchen paper to soak up any excess oil. Repeat the process twice more to make 12 hash browns.

To serve, toss the mackerel flakes and spinach together. Divide between four plates and dress the sides with the grilled garden eggs and hash browns. Drizzle over some chilli oil and serve.

HIBISCUS AND SUMAC PRAWNS

My friend, Tokunbo, makes the best suya prawns you could ever imagine, but not wanting to include too many suya recipes, I used hibiscus and sumac for my version. Sumac is used more in North Africa than West Africa but the flavour of it pairs so well with hibiscus as they both have zesty undertones.

PREP TIME: 5 MINS
COOKING TIME: 10 MINS
SERVES: 4

2 tbsp coconut oil, melted,
   plus extra for frying
2 tbsp freshly squeezed
   lemon juice
1 tsp crushed chilli flakes
1 tsp onion granules
1 tsp ground ginger
1 tsp ground coriander
1 tbsp fine-cut dried hibiscus
   petals
1 tbsp sumac
1 tsp dried tarragon
1 shallot, finely sliced
500g raw king prawns
salt and black pepper

In a small bowl, mix the melted coconut oil, lemon juice, chilli flakes, onion granules, ginger, coriander, hibiscus, sumac and tarragon to form a marinade for the prawns. Add salt and pepper to taste, then coat the prawns evenly with the hibiscus and sumac mix.

Melt the extra coconut oil in a small frying pan over a medium heat and add the shallot. Fry for roughly 3 minutes until the shallot starts to soften. Shake any excess marinade from the prawns before adding to the pan. Cook for roughly 4 minutes, stirring constantly, until cooked through.

Plate the prawns and serve immediately.

GUAVA SALMON CAKES

I don't like buying fishcakes from a store because they can be so easily made at home where you can use an array of different ingredients to really bring the flavour to life. I've used sweet potato as I think it gives a fluffier texture, and I've introduced some guava too which, although popular in Nigeria, isn't often used in cooking in the UK. Sweet and tangy, guava goes perfectly with salmon and adds a lovely tropical twist – fishcakes will never be bland again!

PREP TIME: 20 MINS
PLUS CHILLING TIME
COOKING TIME: 40 MINS
SERVES: 4

600g white-flesh sweet
    potato, peeled and finely
    chopped
½ x 410g tin guava halves in
    syrup, rinsed and drained
105g tin pink salmon,
    drained
2 tsp dried thyme
2 tsp onion granules
1 tsp crushed chilli flakes
1 tsp ground ginger
plain flour, for shaping
2 tbsp coconut oil
lemon wedges, to serve

Rinse the sweet potato and put in a pan of boiling salted water set over a high heat. Cook for 15–20 minutes until soft, then drain in a colander and transfer to a large bowl. Mash the sweet potato until light and fluffy.

In a separate bowl, coarsely crush the guava halves with a fork and add the salmon, thyme, onion granules, chilli flakes and ginger. Mix until well combined, then strain through a sieve to get rid of any extra moisture. Return the mixture to the bowl and add the sweet-potato mash, mixing to combine well. Mould the mixture into 8 cakes, using floured hands, and place in the fridge for 30 minutes until firm.

Melt 1 tablespoon coconut oil in a large frying pan over a medium heat. Fry 4 fishcakes for 5 minutes on each side, until golden and cooked through. Repeat with the remaining tablespoon oil and 4 fishcakes. Serve 2 fishcakes per person, along with a lemon wedge for squeezing over.

EGUSI PRAWN BALLS

Egusi is such a versatile ingredient. I use it in my soups, in slaws and also in this prawn dish because its nutty flavour perfectly complements the saltiness of the dipping sauce. These make a great canapé if you're having people over for dinner – they take very little time to put together and always go down well with my friends.

PREP TIME: 20 MINS
COOKING TIME: 10 MINS
SERVES: 4

330g raw peeled king prawns
1 tsp onion granules
1 tsp celery salt
½ tsp cayenne pepper
1 tsp carob powder
1 tsp groundnut oil, plus
   extra for frying
1 tbsp fine cornmeal
ground egusi, for coating
salt

FOR THE DIP
90g tomato purée
1 tbsp shrimp paste
1 tbsp coconut aminos
   (optional)
2 tbsp onion granules
1 tbsp ground ginger
cayenne pepper
2 tbsp coconut oil, melted

Preheat the oven to 180°C/Gas 4 and line a baking tray with baking paper.

Dry the prawns with kitchen paper before roughly chopping and transferring them to a sieve. Press gently to remove any more excess water, then tip them into a bowl. Add the onion granules, celery salt, cayenne pepper, carob powder and groundnut oil and season with salt. Blitz the prawns into a coarse paste using a hand-held blender, then mix in the cornmeal. Cover with cling film and refrigerate for 1 hour.

Meanwhile, make the dip by whisking together all the ingredients until well combined. Set aside.

Shape the prawn paste into 20 bite-sized balls. Roll each one in the ground egusi, gently pressing in place. Place the balls on the prepared tray and bake for 10 minutes, turning halfway through so that they become brown all over.

Remove from the oven and leave to cool for 5 minutes before serving with the dip.

IJEBU FISH ROLLS

When I used to visit my grandma's house in Ijebu, we would go for strolls around the neighbourhood. The lady who lived behind her sold fish rolls and she often had a long line of people waiting eagerly to buy them. The rolls were crispy and chewy at the same time because the pastry contained yeast but had been deep fried. They were filled with either mackerel or sardines, depending on what she felt like making that day, and they were lightly coated in a rich tomato sauce.

**PREP TIME: 30 MINS
PLUS PROVING TIME
COOKING TIME: 10 MINS
SERVES: 4**

400g plain flour, plus extra
 for dusting
1 tablespoon coconut sugar
 or unrefined brown sugar
½ teaspoon ground nutmeg
1 tsp salt
½ teaspoon fast-action
 dried yeast
1 egg yolk
groundnut oil, for frying

FOR THE FISH FILLING
4 smoked mackerel fillets
2 tbsp tomato purée
1 tsp onion granules
1 tsp dried parsley
1 tsp ground coriander

In a large bowl, mix together the flour, sugar, nutmeg, salt and yeast. Create a well in the centre and add in the egg yolk, along with 200ml water. Use your hands to combine the wet and dry ingredients, gradually bringing in the flour from around the edge of the well, until everything is incorporated into a ball of dough. Turn the dough out on to a lightly floured surface and knead for 5 minutes. Put the dough back into the bowl, cover with cling film and let prove for 30 minutes.

Meanwhile, make the fish filling. In a bowl, break up the mackerel fillets into chunks. Add the tomato purée, onion granules, parsley and coriander, then mix thoroughly so that the mackerel is well coated.

When the dough has finished resting, put it on a lightly floured surface and knock it back to remove any large air bubbles. Divide the dough into 8 pieces and roll out a piece so that it is 2mm thick. Cut off the edges to create a neat rectangle measuring about 10 x 15cm. Spread one-eighth of the mackerel filling down one long edge of the rectangle, leaving 1cm space at the top and bottom. Fold the top and bottom edges in, then roll up tightly like a cigar and press down the long edge to seal. Repeat for the other 7 rolls.

Fill a large saucepan with 4cm of oil and place over a medium heat. The oil is hot enough when a piece of bread dropped into it sizzles immediately. Fry 4 of the fish rolls for 2 minutes. As the bottoms start to brown, flip the rolls over and cook for a further 2 minutes. Use a slotted spoon to remove the rolls and place them on kitchen roll. Repeat with the remaining 4 rolls and leave to cool for 5 minutes before serving.

BAKED AYAMASE TILAPIA ROLL UPS

The first time I was introduced to ayamase, my gut instinct was to run away (as with all things green), but since a lot of my friends at university kept raving on about it, I had to see what the fuss was about. In its raw form, it's pretty much the Nigerian version of pesto but with a kick. After many attempts, I found that palm oil is the essential ingredient that brings this recipe together – you can try another oil but the flavour of the dish won't be the same. Traditionally, Nigerians would use carob powder in its original form (locust beans, known locally as iru) but the powder is much more easily available and can be found in health-food stores. Ayamase goes particularly well with tilapia, which is a firm, flaky fish, mild in flavour and very popular in Nigeria.

PREP TIME: 20 MINS
COOKING TIME: 25 MINS
SERVES: 4

4 large tilapia fillets
2 tbsp coconut oil, melted

FOR THE AYAMASE
2 tbsp palm oil
3 green peppers, chopped
1 Scotch bonnet chilli,
    deseeded (if preferred)
1 green tomato, chopped
    (optional)
1 large onion, chopped
1 tsp carob powder
1 tbsp shrimp paste
1 tsp celery salt
1 tsp black pepper
1 tsp white pepper
2 tsp onion granules
½ tsp turmeric
salt and cayenne pepper

TO SERVE
spinach, wilted
fried puna yam
good-quality chilli oil

Preheat the oven to 180°C/Gas 4.

For the ayamase, add the palm oil to a saucepan set over a medium–high heat. Cover with a lid and leave to smoke for 5 minutes. Remove the pan from the heat and leave to cool without removing the lid.

Add the green peppers, Scotch bonnet, green tomato (if using) and onion to a food processor and roughly blend. Remove the excess moisture by placing the mixture in a nut milk bag and squeezing. Alternatively, this can be done by passing the mixture through a sieve, using the back of a spoon to press out all the excess liquid. Add the carob powder, shrimp paste, spices and smoked palm oil to the mix. Weigh out 60g of the ayamase and set aside for use in the recipe. Any leftover ayamase can be used as a dip or eaten with rice.

Lay out one fillet of tilapia and slice in half lengthways. Spread a generous tablespoon of the ayamase mix over each slice of fish and roll up from the short to the wide end. Place the rolls in a small ovenproof dish with the seam down so that the fish doesn't unravel. Repeat these steps for the remaining fillets.

Brush the rolls with the melted coconut oil and remaining ayamase mix and bake uncovered for about 12–15 minutes, or until the tilapia is opaque and cooked through.

Serve with wilted spinach, fried yam and a generous drizzle of chilli oil.

❀ NOTES

For the best flavour, add onion to the oil during the smoking process. Once the oil has cooled down (but is still liquid), remove the blackened onion and follow recipe as normal. You can easily make the ayamase ahead of time and double the quantity to keep in the fridge for a week or the freezer for a month.

SEARED SCALLOPS IN GRAPEFRUIT SAUCE

Lots of my friends are a bit frightened of cooking scallops but there's really no need to be – they're quick and easy and this dish makes a great starter if you're having a dinner party. The tangy grapefruit juice goes perfectly with the sweetness of the coconut nectar (or honey), and this flavour combination actually goes really well with seafood generally.

PREP TIME: 5 MINS
COOKING TIME: 20 MINS
SERVES: 4

4 tbsp coconut oil, melted
2 shallots, very finely
   chopped
½ Scotch bonnet chilli,
   deseeded and thinly sliced
2cm piece of fresh ginger,
   peeled and finely grated
juice of ½ grapefruit
2 tbsp coconut nectar or
   honey
400g scallops, thawed if
   frozen
salt and cayenne pepper

In a small frying pan set over a medium–low heat, melt 2 tablespoons of the coconut oil and cook the shallots and Scotch bonnet for 2 minutes until soft. Add the ginger, grapefruit juice and coconut nectar or honey. Cook for 5 minutes until the liquid reduces and becomes syrupy. Season with salt and cayenne pepper to taste and set aside.

Pat the scallops dry with kitchen paper. Melt the remaining 2 tablespoons coconut oil in a large frying pan over a medium–high heat. Place half of the scallops in the pan, making sure they don't overlap. Cook for 3 minutes on each side to get a nice golden brown finish. Remove the scallops from the pan and place on a plate, then repeat to cook the second half.

Arrange the scallops on four plates and drizzle with the grapefruit sauce.

MORINGA AND LEMON SCALLOPS

Moringa is thought to have powerful health benefits, so this recipe will appeal to those looking for a healthier lifestyle. In truth, I have used it here as it is commonly used in Hausa dishes, if more frequently with meat than fish. Its flavour is very distinct and varies according to which part of the moringa tree you eat, whether it's the flowers, seeds, pods or roots. The powdered form used in this recipe is made from the leaves and goes really well with scallops. Combined with the Okra and Mango Salad (see page 20), this makes for a great starter.

PREP TIME: 5 MINS
COOKING TIME: 20 MINS
SERVES: 4

400g scallops, thawed if
  frozen
2 tbsp coconut oil, melted
1 shallot, very finely chopped
1 tbsp moringa powder
2 tsp ground ginger
2 tbsp freshly squeezed
  lemon juice
salt and white pepper

Preheat the oven to 180ºC/Gas 4 and line a baking tray with baking paper.

Pat the scallops dry with kitchen paper. In a bowl, mix together the coconut oil, shallot, moringa powder, ginger and lemon juice and season with salt and pepper. Add the scallops and make sure they are well coated with the marinade. Put the scallops on the prepared baking tray and bake for 20 minutes until firm.

Serve the scallops while still hot.

CHARGRILLED SCOTCH SQUID

Nigerian street food is often chargrilled over coals, giving everything a wonderful smoky flavour. Seafood isn't as common as meat in Nigerian cuisine, so this isn't a classic street-food dish, but it would be my addition to the menu! It is quick, fiery and delicious – street food at its best.

PREP TIME: 5 MINS
COOKING TIME: 10 MINS
SERVES: 4

12 squid tubes, thawed if
  frozen
1 tbsp coconut oil, melted
2 Scotch bonnet chillies,
  deseeded (if preferred) and
  finely chopped
1 tsp celery salt
salt, black pepper or
  cayenne pepper
good-quality chilli oil, for
  drizzling

In a bowl, mix together the squid, coconut oil, Scotch bonnets and celery salt.

Set a griddle pan over a medium–high heat. In batches, cook the squid for 2 minutes, turning often with tongs, until the squid has char marks. Once ready, take the squid off the heat quickly.

Season with salt and black pepper or cayenne pepper, and serve drizzled with chilli oil.

CASSAVA STUFFED MUSSELS

My mum's passion for cooking seafood has really influenced me, probably because seafood is so often quick to cook and fuss free. It was her who first introduced me to mussels. Initially I thought they were gross, but once I got used to the texture, I found myself cooking them regularly, in search of their great flavour. The rich, sweet meat of mussels combines really well with tangy, savoury cassava. But if you can't find cassava flour, it's not the end of the world – there are still plenty of interesting flavours going on in this dish.

PREP TIME: 10 MINS
COOKING TIME: 15 MINS
SERVES: 4

1.5kg mussels, debearded
4 tbsp palm oil or coconut oil
½ onion, finely chopped
1 celery stick, finely chopped
2 tbsp cassava flour or
   plain flour
1 tsp ground ginger
2 tbsp palm vinegar or
   white wine vinegar
180ml rice milk
1 tbsp finely chopped baby
   leaf spinach
salt and black pepper

Rinse the mussels in a colander. If any mussels are open, tap them lightly on a hard surface. If they don't close, discard them. Check for any cracked mussels and throw those away too.

Put the mussels in a large pan, pour over 250ml water and bring to the boil. Once boiling, put the lid on and cook the mussels for 4–5 minutes. When the mussels open up, remove from the heat to cool. Once the mussels are cool enough to handle, remove the meat from the shells and chop roughly. Keep half of the mussel shells and discard the rest.

Melt the palm oil or coconut oil in a saucepan over a medium–low heat and fry the onion and celery for 5 minutes. Add the flour and ginger and cook until a paste forms. Add the vinegar and stir in before gradually adding the rice milk. Keep stirring and cook for a few minutes until the sauce begins to thicken. Take off the heat and mix in the spinach and the cooked mussels, and season to taste with salt and pepper.

Spoon the mussels and sauce into the reserved mussel shells and serve.

PEANUT AND GARRI CALAMARI RINGS

My friend Abigail, who provided the inspired banana bread recipe for this book, has an obsession with calamari, which is how I came to try it. So I have two things to thank her for. I have added my own twists to this recipe, using garri instead of breadcrumbs and including peanut butter in the coating for the squid. For me, peanut butter is almost like an African mustard – added liberally to recipes or used as a condiment, it's a key ingredient in Nigerian cooking.

PREP TIME: 20 MINS
COOKING TIME: 10 MINS
SERVES: 4

400g squid rings, thawed if
    frozen
50g cassava flour or plain
    flour
1 tbsp roasted peanut flour
2 eggs, lightly beaten
4 tsp peanut butter or cashew
    butter
110g garri
100g dried breadcrumbs
groundnut oil, for deep frying
salt and black pepper

FOR THE DIPPING SAUCE
4 tbsp coconut cream
1 tsp freshly squeezed lemon
    juice
2 tsp chopped efirin or basil
    leaves
1 tsp onion granules
½ tsp celery salt

To make the dipping sauce, whisk the coconut cream, lemon juice, efirin or basil leaves, onion granules and celery salt until well combined. Taste and adjust the seasoning with salt and black pepper to your liking. Set aside.

Remove any moisture from the squid rings by patting them dry with kitchen paper. Gather three small bowls for your assembly line. In the first bowl combine the cassava flour with the peanut flour and cayenne pepper. In the second bowl mix the eggs and peanut butter or cashew butter until well combined. To the last bowl add the garri and breadcrumbs along with some salt and pepper. Coat the calamari rings in the flour mix and shake off any excess. Next, one at a time, dip them into the egg blend, letting the excess drip off, then coat in the garri mixture.

Fill a medium saucepan two-thirds full with groundnut oil and turn the heat to medium–high. Once the oil is hot, cook half of the coated rings for 2 minutes until light golden. Using a slotted spoon, transfer the cooked calamari to a plate lined with kitchen paper. Repeat to cook the other half of the squid, letting the oil heat back up between batches.

Divide the calamari between four plates and serve with the dipping sauce.

TUNA SKEWERS WITH OVEN-BAKED PLANTAIN WEDGES

My mum used to make these skewers for birthday parties when I was younger. Not only do the flavours of the tuna and the fruits pair really well, but they are also really fun to make – like assembling a rainbow on a stick!

**PREP TIME: 25 MINS
   PLUS MARINATING TIME
COOKING TIME: 30 MINS
SERVES: 4**

240g tuna steak, chopped
   into 2cm cubes
¼ large red onion, chopped
1 red or orange pepper,
   chopped into 2cm cubes
1 small mango or papaya,
   peeled, pitted and chopped
   into 2cm cubes
½ small pineapple, peeled
   and chopped into 2cm
   cubes
1 kiwi, peeled, halved and
   sliced

FOR THE MARINADE
2 tbsp groundnut oil
1 tbsp freshly squeezed
   lemon juice
4cm piece of fresh ginger,
   peeled and finely grated
1 Scotch bonnet chilli,
   deseeded (if preferred) and
   finely chopped
1 tsp onion granules
1 tsp ground ginger
1 tsp garlic granules
1 tsp celery salt
1 tsp dried parsley
1 tsp dried tarragon
1 tsp dried thyme
salt and cayenne pepper

Preheat the grill to medium–high (or 180°C on a fan-grill setting) and line a baking tray with foil.

In a large bowl, whisk together all the ingredients for the marinade. Taste for any additional salt or cayenne pepper needed and adjust to taste. Add the tuna to the bowl and coat the chunks in the marinade. Cover with cling film and let the tuna sit in the fridge for 15–20 minutes to marinate. If using wooden skewers, take this time to soak them in water for at least 15 minutes.

Meanwhile, in another large bowl, mix the 2 tablespoons of groundnut oil for the plantain with the nutmeg and season with salt and cayenne pepper. Top and tail the plantains then peel off the skin. Slice the plantains diagonally into thick slices, then halve each slice. Put the plantain in the nutmeg oil and toss until each wedge is evenly coated. Place the plantain wedges on the prepared baking tray, leaving one side free for the tuna skewers, and grill for 20 minutes.

Once the tuna has finished marinating, take it out of the fridge and begin to assemble your skewers. Grab your first skewer and thread on a chunk of the tuna, followed by 2 squares of red onion, 2 squares of pepper, 1 mango cube and 1 pineapple cube, repeat again and then as you near the end, cap with a few slices of kiwi. Continue the same pattern for the rest of the skewers. This makes 4 packed skewers, but you could space them out to produce 6 or 8.

Take the baking tray out from under the grill and place the skewers in their allocated space. Put the skewers under the grill, along with the plantain, and grill for 8 minutes. You'll need to flip the skewers halfway. Once ready, the tuna should no longer be pink and if cut into should flake easily. The plantains will be golden brown.

FOR THE PLANTAIN WEDGES
2 tbsp groundnut oil
2 tsp nutmeg
2 yellow plantains
crushed peanuts or cashew
  nuts, to serve (optional)

Plate the skewers and the plantain wedges. Sprinkle the wedges with the crushed peanuts and serve.

OSUN'S SOLE

Like the Stacked Shango Beef Steak (see page 146), this recipe is inspired by Yoruba mythology. Osun is known as the goddess of sweet waters and love. She's usually depicted wearing yellow clothing and accessories. To encapsulate her, I've used carob to add sweetness and mango because it's believed to be an aphrodisiac; plus both are yellow in colour, in tribute to Osun's attire. As she's a water goddess, I felt it only appropriate to use fish and sole works particularly well with the flavours of this dish.

PREP TIME: 5 MINS
COOKING TIME: 15 MINS
SERVES: 4

coconut oil, for greasing
4 lemon sole fillets
1 tsp celery salt
1 tbsp carob powder
4cm piece of fresh ginger,
  peeled and grated
1 Scotch bonnet chilli,
  deseeded (if preferred) and
  chopped
1 mango, finely chopped
salt, black pepper and
  cayenne pepper
boiled yams, to serve
  (optional)
roughly chopped coriander,
  to serve (optional)

Preheat the oven to 180°C/Gas 4. Line an oven dish with baking paper and lightly grease with coconut oil.

Place the sole fillets in the oven dish and sprinkle with the celery salt and carob powder. Season with salt and black and cayenne peppers and top with the grated ginger, Scotch bonnet and mango. Bake for 15 minutes, until the sole is golden and comes apart easily with a fork.

Serve each fillet on a plate with yams and sprinkled with coriander, if you like. Enjoy hot!

ATAMA LOBSTER TAILS

Yoruba people tend to eat quite a lot of meat and poultry, despite the wide range of seafood at their disposal. There were very few restaurants in Lagos, that I was aware of, that were dedicated to just seafood so I gave props to the one or two that served lobster. For the most part the lobster they served was grilled on an open flame and coated in a heavy tomato sauce. For a lighter and more simple approach, this recipe makes use of coconut oil and tarragon leaves. This recipe draws inspiration from the Efik people in Nigeria who use a leaf called atama. Atama is a Nigerian herb similar in taste to tarragon and it is used in most of the seafood dishes created by the Efik people.

PREP TIME: 35 MINS
COOKING TIME: 10 MINS
SERVES: 4

120g coconut oil, melted
2 tbsp fresh atama or
 tarragon leaves, chopped
½ white onion or 1 shallot,
 finely chopped
1 Scotch bonnet chilli,
 deseeded (if preferred) and
 finely chopped
4 lobster tails, thawed if
 frozen
groundnut oil, for brushing
2 tsp celery salt
salt and cayenne pepper
lemon wedges, for serving

Preheat the grill to high.

Thoroughly combine the coconut oil, atama or tarragon leaves, onion or shallot, Scotch bonnet and salt and cayenne pepper in a small bowl. Cover with cling film and place in the fridge.

Using kitchen scissors, cut lengthways down the middle of the lobsters, to cut the shell along the belly, stopping before you reach the fan at the bottom. Spread the shell apart using your thumbs. Starting at the thicker end of the tail, gently separate the flesh from the shell using the handle of a teaspoon. Prise the meat away, but be sure to leave the flesh attached at the narrow end of the tail. Rest the meat inside the shell.

Brush the tails with groundnut oil and season with celery salt, plus any extra salt to taste. When the grill is ready, grill the lobster tails, flesh side down, for roughly 4 minutes until the shells turn bright red. Flip the tails over using tongs and if necessary, readjust the lobster flesh. Spoon over the atama coconut oil and cook the lobster meat for roughly a further 4 minutes until firm and white throughout.

Remove from the grill and serve with more atama oil and lemon wedges.

PRAWN CURRY

Tanya, my friend from Sri Lanka, once invited me over for a study session. Her mum was kind enough to offer a fish curry with rice and wanted to know if I'd be needing a knife and fork. Not a surprising question as eating with our hands is something that's done in Nigerian culture too. There is something about eating with hands that makes food ten times more enjoyable — I reckon it's the feeling of freedom and knowing not a single drop is going to waste. While this isn't the exact curry we ate, the inspiration for this Nigerian-style curry came from those memories. It really delivers on flavour as the fragrant efirin goes so well with the prawns. It's a great, simple dish for when family or friends turn up unexpectedly, which has happened quite a bit since mine discovered that I was writing a cookbook!

PREP TIME: 20 MINS
COOKING TIME: 30 MINS
SERVES: 4

2 tbsp palm oil or coconut oil
2 bay leaves
1 onion or 2 shallots, finely
    sliced
2 green peppers, finely
    chopped
2 celery sticks, finely
    chopped
4cm piece of fresh ginger,
    peeled and finely grated
1 tsp ground cloves
4 uda pods (optional)
1 tbsp carob powder
1 tbsp cumin
2 tbsp coriander
1 tbsp turmeric
1 tbsp paprika
2 tsp shrimp paste or coconut
    aminos
2 Scotch bonnet chillies,
    deseeded (if preferred) and
    finely chopped
1 tbsp finely chopped efirin
    or basil
400ml tin coconut milk
400ml fish stock
400g raw king prawns
salt and cayenne pepper
cooked brown short-grain
    rice, to serve

Heat the oil in a large heavy-based frying pan over a medium–high heat. Add the bay leaves, onion or shallots, peppers, celery and ginger and fry for 4 minutes until the onions are soft. Add the spices, shrimp paste or coconut aminos, Scotch bonnets and efirin or basil. Stir for roughly 5 minutes until the oil starts to separate from the paste and the smell of the spices roams around the kitchen.

In a large measuring jug, combine the coconut milk and fish stock, then add to the pan and increase the heat to high. Just before the curry begins to bubble, bring the heat down to low and let simmer for roughly 8 minutes until the liquid has reduced and the peppers and celery have softened. Taste for seasoning and add any salt or cayenne pepper you think it needs. Add the prawns to the pan, cover and cook for a further 8 minutes or so until they are no longer translucent.

Ladle the curry into bowls and serve hot with brown rice.

SPICY GRILLED TILAPIA

I was served something similar to this in a Brixton restaurant, where the chefs used whole fish that they bathed in a paste of spicy peppers. Mine still has a seriously spicy kick, but I have used fillets, which makes it that little bit smarter and less fussy to eat, so great for a dinner party. Tilapia is commonly eaten in Nigeria, but if you can't find it, lemon sole fillets make a good substitute.

PREP TIME: 20 MINS
PLUS MARINATING TIME
COOKING TIME: 15 MINS
SERVES: 4

4 tilapia fillets
a mix of deseeded and thinly
  sliced red, yellow and
  orange peppers, to serve

FOR THE MARINADE
1 fish stock cube, crumbled
1 tsp ground cloves
1 tsp turmeric
1 tbsp groundnut oil
salt, white pepper and
  cayenne pepper

FOR THE SAUCE
½ large onion, chopped
1 red pepper, deseeded and
  chopped
2 celery sticks, chopped
4cm piece of fresh ginger,
  peeled and chopped
2 Scotch bonnet chillies,
  deseeded (if preferred)

In a small bowl, mix the crumbled stock cube, cloves and turmeric with the groundnut oil and season with salt and white and cayenne peppers. Coat the tilapia fillets with the marinade and cover with cling film. Marinate in the fridge for at least 2 hours, or overnight.

When you're almost ready to take the fish out of the fridge, preheat the grill to medium–high (or 180ºC on a fan-grill setting) and line a baking tray with foil.

Put the onion, pepper, celery, ginger and Scotch bonnets in a blender. Add 60ml water and blitz to a wet purée.

Place the fish on the lined baking tray and coat generously with the onion and pepper blend. Transfer to the grill and cook for about 15 minutes or until cooked through and flaky.

Plate the fish and serve topped with some of the sliced peppers.

BAKED KULI KULI COD WITH CAYENNE YAM CHIPS

I've always been a big fan of fish and chips. On my walk home from lectures at university, I would always be so tempted by the smells coming from the local chippy. I usually gave in once every fortnight or so because I couldn't resist the temptation of the crispy batter and vinegar-soaked chips. Incorporating the flavours of roasted peanuts and spicy cayenne pepper, this is my Nigerian take on a British classic.

**PREP TIME: 15 MINS
   PLUS RESTING TIME
COOKING TIME: 45 MINS
SERVES: 4**

groundnut oil, for greasing
4 cod loin fillets
1 large egg
200ml buttermilk (or ½ x
   400g tin coconut milk mixed
   with 1 tbsp lemon juice)
lemon wedges, to serve

FOR THE DRY BRINE
2 tbsp dried dill
2 tbsp dried parsley
2 tbsp onion granules
2 tbsp celery salt
2 tsp flaky sea salt

FOR THE KULI KULI FLOUR
160g plain flour
4 tbsp roasted peanut flour
2 tbsp cornflour
3 tsp onion granules
2 tsp ginger
2 tsp salt
2 tsp cayenne pepper

FOR THE YAM CHIPS
800g puna yam, peeled and
   sliced into thick-cut chips
2 tbsp coconut oil, melted
2 tbsp cassava flour or plain flour
1 tsp cayenne pepper
1 tsp coarsely ground black
   pepper

Preheat the oven to 180°C/Gas 4. Line an oven dish with baking paper. Grease the baking paper lightly with groundnut oil.

Combine all the dry brine ingredients on a plate. Coat each cod fillet in the dry brine, shaking off any excess, and transfer to a clean plate. Cover with cling film and leave to rest in the fridge for 30 minutes while you prepare the yam chips.

Bring a large pan of water to the boil, add the yams and cook for 5 minutes. Drain in a colander and tip on to a baking tray, then brush the yam chips with the melted coconut oil.

In a bowl, mix the cassava or plain flour, cayenne pepper and black pepper. Add the boiled yam chips and toss until they're evenly coated. Return the chips to the baking tray before roasting in the preheated oven for 40 minutes, until crisp.

While the chips are in the oven, return to the fish. On a plate, make the kuli kuli flour by combining all the ingredients. In a large dish, whisk together the egg and buttermilk until well combined. One fillet at time, dunk the cod into the buttermilk mix and let the excess drip off before coating evenly in the kuli kuli flour and transferring to the prepared oven dish. Bake the cod for 15 minutes, until golden and firm.

Serve the cod with the yam chips and lemon wedges.

LEMON AND THYME SEA BASS WITH GARDEN EGG CROQUETTES

Lemon and thyme are classic accompaniments to sea bass – simple but delicious. Unsurprisingly, I like to add a few twists: a little cayenne pepper on the fish for added fieriness and a serving of golden garden egg croquettes on the side. Crispy and creamy, croquettes are super simple to make and I really advocate using garden eggs (or aubergines as an alternative) rather than just the standard potato. They give a lovely silky texture, which goes so well with the crispiness of the fried garri.

PREP TIME: 25 MINS
COOKING TIME: 30 MINS
SERVES: 4

8 sprigs of thyme
4 sea bass fillets
1 tbsp coconut oil, melted
1 shallot, finely chopped
1 lemon, zested and juiced
salt and cayenne pepper

FOR THE CROQUETTES
6 small garden eggs or
 2 chopped aubergines
150g puna yam, peeled and
 finely chopped
2 eggs, plus 1 egg yolk,
 beaten
2 tbsp coconut cream
2 tbsp peanut butter
1 shallot, finely chopped
1 celery sticks, finely
 chopped
1 Scotch bonnet chilli,
 deseeded and finely
 chopped
50g garri
50g breadcrumbs
500ml groundnut oil

Bring a pan of water to the boil over a high heat. Turn the heat down to medium and add the garden eggs and puna yam. Let cook for 10 minutes until the garden eggs are soft and the yam can easily be pierced with a fork. Drain the garden eggs and yam and set aside to cool.

Separate the flesh of the garden eggs from their skins and put the flesh in a large bowl, along with the yam. Mash the two together with the back of a fork, then add the beaten egg yolk, coconut cream, peanut butter, shallot, celery and Scotch bonnet. Season to taste with salt and cayenne pepper. Roll into balls about the size of golf balls and chill for 1 hour, or until firm.

Meanwhile, line a colander with kitchen paper and preheat the oven to 180°C/Gas 4.

Once the balls have firmed up, beat the 2 eggs in a bowl and add the garri and breadcrumbs to another bowl. Dip a ball into the beaten egg, let the excess drip off, then roll into the garri/breadcrumb mix. Repeat until all the balls are coated. Heat up the groundnut oil in a large saucepan. When the oil is hot enough, the garri/breadcrumb mix will sizzle immediately. Fry the balls for about 3 minutes on one side until golden, then flip over and fry for a further 2 minutes on the other side. Work in batches, frying a quarter of the balls at a time, and remove from the pan with a slotted spoon. Drain in the prepared colander and set aside to cool.

While the croquettes are cooking, put the thyme in a large casserole dish and top with the sea bass fillets. Sprinkle the fillets with some salt and cayenne pepper. In a small bowl, mix together the coconut oil, shallot and lemon zest and juice, then pour it over the fillets. Bake for 10 minutes, or until the fish is cooked through.

To serve, plate the sea bass fillets, divide the croquettes evenly between the plates and enjoy.

STICKY PINEAPPLE COD

I know some people find the idea of eating pineapple alongside meat (gammon, for example) a little bizarre, but its sweet, tangy flavour goes really well with white fish. I've used cod, but any variety will work just as well. Definitely don't forget the lemon here, as a squeeze of sharpness brings everything together.

PREP TIME: 15 MINS
COOKING TIME: 20 MINS
SERVES: 4

2 tbsp groundnut oil
4 cod fillets or loins
½ x 435g tin crushed
   pineapple, drained
1 Scotch bonnet chilli,
   deseeded (if preferred) and
   finely chopped
4 tbsp coconut water
1 tbsp coconut nectar or
   honey
1 lemon, quartered, to serve
salt, black pepper and
   cayenne pepper

In a frying pan, heat 1 tablespoon of the groundnut oil over a medium heat. Season the cod fillets with salt and the peppers and, cooking two at a time, fry them for roughly 3 minutes on each side. Once cooked through, the cod should be an opaque white throughout, while the top and bottom are golden brown. Transfer to a plate and set aside.

Pour the second tablespoon of oil into the frying pan and add the crushed pineapple, Scotch bonnet, coconut water and coconut nectar or honey. Let cook for 2–3 minutes until the mixture begins to bubble. Return the cod loins to the pan to warm up again.

To serve, place each fillet on a plate and cover with the pineapple sauce. Enjoy hot with a lemon wedge to squeeze over.

PALM OIL HALIBUT BAKED IN UMA LEAVES

I try to make presentation one of my priorities when I'm cooking, and using uma or banana leaves to serve these halibut fillets looks really smart and is a guaranteed way to impress your guests. Because halibut is such a meaty fish, it takes on flavour really well and can stand up to the Scotch bonnet in this recipe. Although it's always been a family favourite, it was only actually quite recently that I discovered how versatile halibut is, so I'd recommend experimenting with it if cooking fish scares you a little.

PREP TIME: 15 MINS
COOKING TIME: 15 MINS
SERVES: 4

4 uma leaves or banana
   leaves (optional)
coconut oil, for greasing
4 halibut fillets
1 tbsp carob powder
2 tsp shrimp paste or coconut
   aminos
1 Scotch bonnet chilli,
   deseeded (if preferred) and
   finely chopped
½ red onion, chopped
4 tbsp palm oil or coconut
   oil, melted
100ml fish stock
salt and cayenne pepper
rice, to serve

Preheat the oven to 180°C/Gas 4. If using, cut the uma or banana leaves into 4 squares, each big enough for a halibut fillet to sit on. Lightly grease a casserole dish and the uma leaves with coconut oil. If you don't have uma or banana leaves, just grease the dish well so that the fish doesn't stick.

Sprinkle the halibut fillets with salt and cayenne pepper.

In a blender, combine the carob powder, shrimp paste, Scotch bonnet, onion, palm oil or coconut oil and fish stock into a watery paste. Spread the mixture evenly over the fillets and place each one on top of an uma or banana leaf inside the casserole dish. Bake for 15 minutes until the fish is firm and baked all the way through.

Plate the fish with the uma or banana leaves beneath, if using, and serve with some rice. Enjoy hot.

BAOBAB TROUT

Trout is a really tasty fish that goes particularly well with robust flavours, which is why I've paired it with this zesty baobab paste. When I was growing up we rarely ate trout, so now I usually save it for special occasions. For more day-to-day dinners, I use salmon instead and it's just as tasty. Serve with a scattering of toasted egusi seeds — their nuttiness really brings the dish together.

PREP TIME: 10 MINS
COOKING TIME: 10 MINS
SERVES: 4

1 tbsp coconut oil
½ onion, thinly sliced
1 Scotch bonnet chilli,
    deseeded (if preferred) and
    finely chopped
4 trout fillets
salt and cayenne pepper
toasted egusi seeds or flaked
    almonds, to serve

FOR THE BAOBAB PASTE
4 tsp coconut nectar or honey
1 tsp tomato purée
1 tbsp freshly squeezed
    lemon juice
2 tbsp baobab powder

In a small bowl, whisk together the coconut nectar or honey, tomato purée, lemon juice and baobab powder to form a paste. Set aside.

In a large frying pan over a medium–high heat, melt the coconut oil and fry the onion and Scotch bonnet for 4 minutes, stirring constantly. Sprinkle the trout fillets with salt and cayenne pepper, then add them to the pan and cook for 4 minutes on each side. Transfer the fillets to plates, along with the onions and Scotch bonnet.

Add the baobab paste and 80ml water to the frying pan and stir together. Let cook for 1–2 minutes, stirring constantly, until thickened. Pour the glaze over the trout and sprinkle with the toasted egusi seeds or flaked almonds. Serve hot.

Meat and Poultry

MUM'S GRILLED CHICKEN DRUMSTICKS

Agie Iya Lopè (Yoruba)

In Yoruba culture, parents aren't called by their first names. Rather, they're referred to as the mother or father of their firstborn — so in my mother's case, Iya Lopè. Her approach to cooking has always been to create quick and easy dishes. When I was younger, we would go to the local video store on a Saturday night and choose a film to watch. When we got home, she would find whatever spices she could and create seasoning for chicken drumsticks to eat as we watched. No matter what she added, they were always so appetizing. She said her secret was to add lemon juice to the marinade, but I suspect there's more to it than that.

PREP TIME: 5 MINS
COOKING TIME: 35 MINS
SERVES: 4

12 chicken drumsticks
parsley leaves, to serve

FOR MUM'S MARINADE
1 tbsp coconut aminos
1 tbsp tamarind paste
1 tbsp freshly squeezed
   lemon juice
2 tsp onion granules
1 tsp garlic granules
1 tsp paprika
1 tsp celery salt
1 tsp ground cumin
1 tsp dried thyme
1 tsp dried sage
salt and cayenne pepper

Preheat the oven to 210°C/Gas 6–7 and line a baking tray with baking paper.

In a small bowl, mix together the aminos, tamarind paste, lemon juice, onion and garlic granules, paprika, celery salt and cumin. Add the herbs to the marinade and taste for salt and cayenne pepper. Place the drumsticks into a large bowl and toss through the marinade. Once the chicken is well coated, place on to the baking tray and bake in the oven for 30–35 minutes, flipping over halfway.

When the chicken is well browned, and when pierced the juices run clear, sprinkle with parsley and enjoy while hot. If you have the patience, wait 5 minutes to allow the chicken to rest before digging in.

HIBISCUS CHICKEN

I find it quite odd that hibiscus is mainly used for drinks in Nigeria and isn't incorporated into more cooking. For me, hibiscus is to West Africa as sakura is to East Asia, or rose is to the Middle East. Hibiscus tastes quite similar to cranberry and when I'm looking to have something vibrant, I turn to this recipe. The flavour of the chicken is quite rich, so I recommend pairing it with a salad or rice boiled in coconut milk, and dressing simply with fresh parsley. Dried hibiscus petals can be found in most African and Caribbean stores, or online.

PREP TIME: 20 MINS
   PLUS MARINATING TIME
COOKING TIME: 30 MINS
SERVES: 4

4 chicken breasts
2 tbsp coconut oil, melted
fine-cut dried hibiscus petals,
   to serve
Fried Coconut Rice (page
   51), to serve

FOR THE MARINADE
1 tsp celery salt
1 tsp onion granules
1 tsp garlic granules
1 tsp black pepper
1 tsp ground white pepper
1 tsp cayenne pepper
2 tsp finely chopped parsley
2 tsp finely chopped tarragon

FOR THE SAUCE
2 tbsp freshly squeezed
   lemon juice
200ml unsweetened coconut
   water
2 tbsp fine-cut dried hibiscus
   petals
4 tbsp coconut sugar

In a large bowl, combine all the marinade ingredients. Toss in the chicken breasts and coconut oil, mix so that the chicken is well coated and leave to marinate for 30 minutes.

To make the sauce, whisk the lemon juice, coconut water, hibiscus and coconut sugar in a small saucepan over a medium heat. Bring to the boil before reducing the heat to low, then leave to simmer for 15 minutes until the liquid has reduced by half. Set aside and allow the sauce to cool completely for roughly 15 minutes, until it thickens.

Put a griddle pan over a medium heat to heat up, and meanwhile brush each marinated chicken breast with the sauce. Place them in the hot pan and cook, giving each side 4–5 minutes before turning – they should be nicely browned and cooked throughout.

Plate the chicken and drizzle over any of the remaining hibiscus sauce. Sprinkle over some crushed hibiscus petals and serve with fried coconut rice on the side.

❀ NOTES

This is a great dish for a date night in and you could easily swap the chicken for duck breast to make it that little bit more special.

MALT-GLAZED CHICKEN WINGS

Non-alcoholic malt drinks are very popular in Nigeria and West African culture. They come in beer-shaped bottles and made me feel very mature when I drank them as a child. For people who haven't grown up drinking malt drinks, the taste is a bit like Marmite – you either love it or you hate it. None the less, I wanted to include a malt recipe in this book, so here is a deliciously sweet glaze for chicken wings. Serve with roughly chopped carrots, celery and sour cream, or they're brilliant on their own if you don't fancy the extra work.

PREP TIME: 15 MINS
   PLUS MARINATING TIME
COOKING TIME: 30 MINS
SERVES: 4

12 chicken wings
2 tsp onion granules
2 tsp ground ginger
2 tsp celery salt

FOR THE MALT GLAZE
2 tbsp coconut oil, melted
1 tbsp coconut aminos
4 tbsp malt extract
4 tbsp coconut nectar or
   honey
salt and cayenne pepper

Preheat the oven to 180°C/Gas 4 and line a baking tray with baking paper.

In a large bowl, season the chicken wings with the onion granules, ground ginger and celery salt. Leave to sit for 15 minutes.

In a smaller bowl, mix the coconut oil, coconut aminos, malt extract and coconut nectar or honey. Taste and season with salt and cayenne pepper. Brush the wings with the malt glaze and place them on the baking tray.

Cook the wings in the preheated oven for 15 minutes before turning and cooking for a further 15 minutes. Once ready, the wings will be a dark glossy brown and there should be no pink flesh. The tips of the wings may burn slightly, but it's nothing to worry about.

Allow the wings to cool slightly before serving.

AMINA'S CHICKEN

Kaza Amina (Hausa)

Amina was a queen, legendary to Hausa people for fighting in numerous battles in what could be called Medieval Africa. The concept of Hunter's Chicken (introduced to me by Sean, a friend from university) inspired me to create something similar in Amina's honour. Where Hunter's Chicken plays with sweet and salty tastes, Nigerians are more accustomed to spicy, savoury flavourings — hence the added fieriness in my version, as befits a true warrior. As most Hausa people don't eat bacon for religious reasons, I've used turkey bacon in this recipe, however feel free to use regular bacon if you like.

PREP TIME: 10 MINS
COOKING TIME: 35 MINS
SERVES: 4

4 chicken breasts
2 tsp onion granules
1 tsp celery salt
1 tsp finely ground white pepper
½ tsp ground turmeric
125g mozzarella cheese
8 slices of unsmoked turkey bacon

FOR THE WARRIOR SAUCE
1 tbsp groundnut oil
1 onion, finely chopped
250g mushrooms, thinly sliced
500ml rice milk
1 chicken stock cube
1 fresh bay leaf
2 sprigs of thyme
2 tbsp cornflour
salt and cayenne pepper

Preheat the oven to 180°C/Gas 4, line 4 small oval casserole dishes with foil and soak 8 cocktail sticks.

To make the sauce, in a small saucepan heat the groundnut oil and cook the onions and mushrooms for 5–6 minutes on medium–high heat until the onions have softened and the mushrooms have shrunk in size. Pour in the rice milk and add the chicken stock cube. Season to taste with salt and cayenne pepper, then add in the bay leaf and thyme sprigs. Bring to the boil, then reduce the heat to low and let simmer for a further 3 minutes.

Mix the cornflour with 6 tablespoons water and pour into the sauce, stirring until well combined. Cook for a further 2 minutes until thickened, then adjust the flavour with extra salt if necessary. Once the sauce has thickened, cover and set aside.

Make a 3–4cm-deep incision down the length of a chicken breast to create a pocket, leaving 2cm uncut at the top and bottom of the breast. Repeat the process for the other 3 breasts.

In a small bowl, combine the onion granules, celery salt, white pepper and turmeric. Lay a chicken breast out and coat it in the spice mix. Stuff the pocket with mozzarella slices, then tightly wrap the breast with 2 rashers of turkey bacon and secure with cocktail sticks. Repeat for the other 3 breasts.

Place each breast in a casserole dish and pour over the sauce, making sure to distribute it evenly. Cover the dishes with foil and cook in the preheated oven for 15 minutes. Take the foil off the dishes and cook for a further 10 minutes, so that the chicken is nice and browned. To check if it is cooked, pierce the thickest part of the meat with a fork and the juices should run clear.

Carefully remove the toothpicks from the chicken and let cool for 5 minutes before serving.

ROAST GRAPEFRUIT AND TURMERIC CHICKEN

Grapefruit is eaten regularly in Nigeria, at all times of the day. Since it goes particularly well with turmeric, which is used to add colour to a number of Nigerian dishes, this recipe is really evocative to me. I love pairing poultry with citrus fruits because of their lovely sharp flavours, and this roast chicken will leave your kitchen smelling deliciously sweet – almost as though you're baking a cake.

PREP TIME: 10 MINS
  PLUS MARINATING TIME
COOKING TIME: 1 HOUR
  30 MINS
SERVES: 4

1.8kg whole chicken
2 grapefruits, peeled and
  sliced

FOR THE MARINADE
2 tbsp palm wine vinegar or
  white wine vinegar
2 tbsp coconut oil, melted
2 tbsp coconut nectar or
  honey
juice of ½ red grapefruit
1 tsp crushed chilli flakes
8 sprigs of thyme
2 bay leaves

FOR THE RUB
1 chicken stock cube
2 tbsp coconut sugar or
  unrefined brown sugar
1 tbsp turmeric
2 tsp carob powder
1 tsp ground ginger

To make the marinade, whisk together the vinegar, coconut oil, coconut nectar or honey, grapefruit juice and chilli flakes in a bowl. Place the whole chicken into a ziplock bag and pour in the marinade. Add the sprigs of thyme and bay leaves. Seal the bag and marinate for at least 2 hours, or overnight, if possible.

Preheat the oven to 180°C/Gas 4 and lightly oil a roasting tray.

Place the grapefruit slices in the tray. Remove the chicken from the ziplock bag and place on top of the grapefruit slices, pouring over the juices from the marinade.

In a small bowl, make the rub by mixing together the crumbled stock cube, sugar, turmeric, carob powder and ginger. Sprinkle the spice mix evenly over the chicken. Add salt and pepper to your liking.

Roast the chicken in the preheated oven for about 1½ hours, until cooked through. To check if it is cooked, pierce the thickest part of the meat with a fork and the juices should run clear.

❀ NOTES
It's important to peel the grapefruit as the skin has a bitter aftertaste.

PUMPKIN SOUP WITH TURKEY

Miyan Taushe (Hausa)

Unlike most Nigerian soups, this one is on the sweeter side and is perfect for those autumn months when pumpkin (tausha in Hausa) comes into season. We always used to save the pumpkin seeds to make Egusi Soup (Obe Egusi – see page 18). This soup reminds me of Ghana's infamous groundnut soup, which is also served with soft, sticky rice balls. Coconut oil can be used instead of palm oil, but the flavour of the dish won't quite be the same.

PREP TIME: 20 MINS
COOKING TIME: 35 MINS
SERVES: 4

2 tbsp palm oil
400g turkey, diced
1 onion, chopped
2 salad tomatoes, chopped
1 yellow pepper, deseeded
   and finely chopped
160g deseeded, peeled and
   chopped pumpkin or
   butternut squash
1 Scotch bonnet chilli,
   deseeded (if preferred) and
   chopped
2 tbsp peanut flour
1 tbsp carob powder
800ml chicken stock
100g spinach, chopped
1 tbsp freshly squeezed
   lemon juice
salt and cayenne pepper

Black Rice Balls (Tuwo
   Shinkafa Bak'i – page 45),
   to serve

Melt the palm oil in a large saucepan over a medium heat and cook the turkey for about 5 minutes, stirring occasionally, until it is browned on all sides. Remove the turkey from the pan with a slotted spoon and set aside on a plate. To the same pan add the onion, tomatoes, pepper, pumpkin or butternut squash and Scotch bonnet. Fry for roughly 5 minutes until the onions start to soften.

Stir in the peanut flour and carob powder and cook for a further 2 minutes. Add the chicken stock to pan while stirring and bring the mix to a boil. Once bubbling, turn down the heat to low and allow to simmer for 10 minutes, or until the vegetables are completely soft.

Use a hand-held blender to blend the soup until smooth. Add the cooked turkey back into the pot along with the spinach and lemon juice. Let cook for a further 5 minutes until the soup has thickened. Season to taste with salt and cayenne pepper.

Ladle the soup into 4 bowls and serve with Black Rice Balls (Tuwo Shinkafa Bak'i).

❁ NOTES
Don't throw away the seeds of the pumpkin or squash as they can be used to make Egusi Soup (Obe Egusi – see page 18).

GRILLED NIGERIAN BASIL TURKEY

Efirin Tòlótòló (Yoruba)

Nigerians have a wide range of different herbs that they like to use in their cooking and one of my grandma's favourites is efirin, Nigeria's answer to basil. With an almost minty aroma, it's dark green in colour and has beautiful purple veins running throughout. Efirin goes surprisingly well with turkey, just don't forget to let the meat marinate properly, so that all the flavours are thoroughly infused. Dried efirin is available in international supermarkets or online, but if you can't find it, dried basil is a good substitute.

**PREP TIME: 10 MINS
 PLUS MARINATING TIME
COOKING TIME: 25 MINS
SERVES: 4**

2 tbsp lime juice
1 tbsp coconut oil, melted
4 tbsp groundnut oil, plus
  extra for frying
1 tbsp peanut butter or
  cashew butter
1 tbsp palm wine vinegar or
  white wine vinegar
1 onion, finely chopped
1 tsp onion granules
1 tsp turmeric
1 tsp white pepper
2 tbsp dried efirin or dried
  basil
1 tsp dried mint
4 turkey breast steaks
salt and cayenne pepper
lime wedges, to serve
Onion Millet (page 60), to
  serve

In a small bowl, whisk together all the ingredients, except the turkey steaks, until well combined and season with salt and cayenne pepper. Put the turkey in a ziplock bag, pour the marinade over and coat well. Leave in the fridge to marinate for 1 hour.

Lightly oil a cast-iron griddle and place over a medium–high heat. Two at a time, grill the turkey steaks for 6 minutes on each side. Remove from the grill and let rest.

Plate the basil turkey steaks and serve each with a wedge of lime and some of the onion millet.

DUCK LEGS IN GUAVA SAUCE

Markets in Nigeria can be very intimidating and when I visited them with my family, I was often afraid of getting lost in the swarms of people. I would hold on tightly to my grandma while the women at the stalls would try and convince her to buy their produce. She haggled down their prices majestically, always offering to buy me a treat afterwards. The only things that ever really caught my eye were the fruits on offer. On one occasion, I remember seeing mountains of what I initially thought were small green and yellow apples. It was only when I saw their pink flesh that I realized they were, in fact, guavas. That was the beginning of my love affair with this delicious fruit, which pairs well with duck because of its sweet taste and pear-like texture.

PREP TIME: 15 MINS
COOKING TIME: 40 MINS
SERVES: 4

4 duck legs
salt and cayenne pepper
Nigerian Roasted Veg (page
   35), to serve

FOR THE GUAVA SAUCE
1 tbsp coconut oil
410g tin guava halves in
   syrup, drained and chopped
2 tbsp lime juice
1 tsp whole cloves
1 tsp ground ginger
1 tsp celery salt
2 tbsp guava jam

Preheat the oven to 200°C/Gas 6. Fill a baking tray with a rack halfway with water and place on the middle shelf.

Use kitchen paper to pat the duck legs dry, then sprinkle over some salt and cayenne pepper. Transfer the duck legs on to the wire rack of the oven tray and roast for 40 minutes until cooked through.

While the duck is cooking, set a small saucepan over a high heat and melt the coconut oil. Add the drained guava halves and cook for 5 minutes until they easily break down. Add the rest of the guava sauce ingredients to the saucepan, along with 150ml water and mix together well. Cook for about 7 minutes, until thickened slightly, then take the pan off the heat and use a potato masher to break it down into a coarse purée. Set aside and let cool until the duck legs are ready.

Plate each duck leg on top of a bed of Nigerian roasted veg and drizzle over the desired amount of guava sauce.

KOLA BUTTERFLIED GUINEA FOWL

Kola Ogazi (Igbo)

In Igbo culture, kola nuts represent hospitality. They are used to celebrate the arrival of special guests to a village or town, the union of a couple or the birth of a baby. Unless you're in Nigeria, kola nuts are only available in powdered form or as a notoriously popular fizzy drink. They have quite a kick to them in terms of smell, a strong, bitter aftertaste and are high in caffeine, which means instant coffee is a good substitute for them if you are unable to find them – simply increase the quantity of coffee granules in the recipe to 4 tablespoons.

**PREP TIME: 25 MINS
PLUS COOLING TIME
COOKING TIME: 1 HOUR
15 MINS
SERVES: 4–6**

**2 tbsp kola nut powder
2 tbsp instant coffee granules
2 tbsp coconut oil
6 tbsp coconut sugar or
unrefined brown sugar
2 tbsp groundnut oil
2 guinea fowl
2 onions, quartered
4 celery sticks, chopped
400ml chicken stock
1 lemon, zested and juiced
2 tbsp palm wine vinegar or
white wine vinegar
100g black grapes, halved
2 tsp dried efirin or basil
salt and cayenne pepper**

Preheat the oven to 180°C/Gas 4.

In a small bowl, mix together the kola nut powder, coffee granules, coconut oil and sugar.

Turn a fowl over so that it is breast down, then use kitchen shears to cut down either side of the spine to remove it. Turn the fowl over and press it flat. Repeat for the other fowl. Spread the kola rub all over the fowls, making sure all areas are covered.

Heat 1 tablespoon of the groundnut oil in a frying pan big enough to fit the butterflied fowl. Place a fowl, skin side down, into the pan and let it brown for about 7 minutes, alongside half the onions and celery sticks. Transfer everything to a large roasting tray and repeat for the other fowl and the remaining onions and celery, adding them to the tray, too, once browned.

Add the chicken stock, lemon zest and juice, vinegar, grapes and the dried efirin or basil leaves to the roasting tray and season with salt and cayenne pepper. Transfer the tray to the oven and roast the fowls for about 1 hour until rich brown, basting in the juices every 15 minutes to keep the birds from drying out. When the thickest part of the meat is pierced with a skewer, the juices should run clear.

Let the fowl cool for 10 minutes before cutting up and serving.

PINEAPPLE AND HIBISCUS STUFFED PORK LOIN

Pork is one of those meats that seems to pair perfectly with sweet, tangy fruits and flavours. For me, pineapple and hibiscus are the optimum duo in this respect. The beauty of this dish is how the swirl of the hibiscus and pineapple ripples through the loin. This is the kind of dish I like to make for a Sunday dinner if I want something other than beef or chicken.

PREP TIME: 25 MINS
**COOKING TIME: 1 HOUR
40 MINS**
SERVES: 6

2 tbsp coconut oil
½ onion, finely chopped
2cm piece of fresh ginger,
   finely chopped
2 celery stalks, finely
   chopped
1 tsp ground ginger
1 tsp celery salt
2 sprigs of fresh sage
2 sprigs of fresh thyme
435g tin crushed pineapple
4 tbsp fine-cut dried hibiscus
   petals
40g egusi seeds, toasted
40g garri or breadcrumbs,
   toasted
1.8kg boneless pork loin
groundnut oil, for brushing
salt, black pepper and
   cayenne pepper

Preheat the oven to 180°C/Gas 4.

Heat the coconut oil in a frying pan placed over a medium–low heat and allow to melt. Add the chopped onion, ginger and celery and fry for 5 minutes until softened. Transfer to a bowl and let cool. Once cool add the spices, sage, thyme, pineapple, hibiscus, egusi seeds and garri or breadcrumbs. Mix and season to taste.

Place the pork on a chopping board, fat side down and the short end facing towards you. Slice the loin open down its length, unrolling as you go, so that you are left with a slab of meat about 3cm thick. Cover the pork with cling film and pound flat using a meat mallet or the bottom of a pan.

Coat both sides of the loin with groundnut oil and season with salt, black pepper and cayenne pepper. Spread the pineapple–hibiscus mixture over the pork (the fat should still be facing downwards) making sure to leave 2cm space around the edges. Starting with the short side, tightly roll up the loin, securing the seams with kitchen string.

Lay the pork on a rack on top of a roasting tin and roast for 1 hour and 40 minutes until it is cooked through. To test if the pork is cooked, pierce the roast with a knife – any juices that run out should be clear.

Take the loin out of the oven and allow to rest for 10 minutes. Remove the string from the pork and cut into slices to serve.

PALM WINE PORK CHOPS

Emu Elede (Yoruba)

Palm wine is created from the sap of palm trees. Fresh from the tree it's still a juice, however after two hours or so it becomes alcoholic, and after a day it's turned into a vinegar. It's usually present at Nigerian parties, although palm wine isn't exclusive to Nigeria – it's also consumed in Ghana, South Africa and Asian countries such as Malaysia and Thailand. In this recipe, the palm wine adds a sweetness that really enhances the flavour of the apples. Combined with the bay, thyme and ginger, the end result is a lovely medley of sweet and savoury. Palm wine should be available to buy at most African or Asian restaurants, but, if not, a white wine can be substituted.

PREP TIME: 5 MINS
COOKING TIME: 20 MINS
SERVES: 4

4 pork chops
2 tbsp coconut oil, melted
2 pink lady apples, peeled, cored and chopped
1 onion, halved and thinly sliced
2cm piece of fresh ginger, grated
60ml palm wine or a fruity white wine
60ml coconut water
4 sprigs of thyme
2 bay leaves
salt and black pepper

Brush both sides of each pork chop with coconut oil and sprinkle over some salt and pepper.

Heat a large cast-iron skillet over a medium–high heat. Add the pork chops to the pan and cook for 3 minutes on each side – they should be well browned. Place the pork chops on a plate and set aside.

Add any coconut oil leftover from brushing the pork chops into the pan along with the apples, onion and ginger. Bring the heat down to low and cook for 5–6 minutes until the onions are softened.

Add the palm wine and coconut water to the pan along with the thyme and bay leaves and cook for about 2 minutes. Add the pork chops back into the pan and cook for a further 5 minutes until the sauce is reduced and thickened.

Serve the chops immediately, drizzling over any extra sauce.

NIGERIAN-STYLE MEATBALLS

My favourite meatballs are the Swedish kind, so it was only a matter of time before I gave them a Nigerian makeover. Pork is the perfect mince to complement the array of spices in this recipe. In fact, the meatballs are quite fiery, so the creamy sauce helps mellow the heat. If you fancy a Nigerian-Swedish fusion, serve with Hasselback Plantains (Ogede Inakuna — see page 27), but I find these meatballs quite filling on their own.

PREP TIME: 25 MINS
COOKING TIME: 25–30 MINS
SERVES: 4

400g pork mince
2 egg yolks
1 onion, finely chopped
2cm piece of fresh ginger,
   peeled and finely grated
1 Scotch bonnet chilli,
   deseeded (if preferred) and
   finely chopped
6 tbsp garri
1 tbsp tarragon, finely
   chopped
1 tsp carob powder
1 tsp nutmeg
2–3 tbsp groundnut oil
2 tbsp palm oil or coconut oil
2 tbsp cassava flour or plain
   flour
400ml chicken stock
4 tbsp coconut cream
salt and cayenne pepper
fine-cut dried hibiscus petals,
   to serve

In a large bowl, mix the pork mince, egg yolks, onion, ginger, Scotch bonnet, garri, tarragon, carob powder and nutmeg until well combined. Add salt and cayenne pepper to taste, then shape into 16 evenly sized balls.

Heat 1 tablespoon of the groundnut oil in a large heavy-based frying pan set over a medium heat. In two or three batches, brown the meatballs all over for about 5 minutes. When ready, remove from the pan on to a plate and set aside.

Melt the palm oil or coconut oil in the same pan, then sprinkle over the flour. Slowly add the chicken stock, whisking continuously. Cook for 5 minutes until thickened slightly, then stir in the coconut cream and season to taste with salt and cayenne pepper.

Return the meatballs to the pan to continue cooking for about 10 minutes until the meatballs are cooked through and the sauce has thickened a little more.

To serve, divide the meatballs equally between four plates and sprinkle over the hibiscus petals.

STICKY TAMARIND PORK RIBS

Barbecues are very popular in my family, and a good excuse to get together with my cousins for a catch-up. These ribs are a family favourite and are inspired by Hausa cuisine. The flavours of the rub go really well with the ribs, although this is definitely my take on it; many Hausa people are Muslims, and so wouldn't eat pork, using goat or lamb instead. It's really worth leaving the spice rub on the ribs overnight if possible – the salt and sugar mix tenderizes and improves the flavour of the meat.

**PREP TIME: 10 MINS
PLUS MARINATING
COOKING TIME: 3 HOURS
30 MINS
SERVES: 4**

3 tbsp coconut sugar or
   unrefined brown sugar
2 tbsp roasted peanut flour
1 tsp celery salt
1 tsp onion granules
2 racks baby back pork ribs
4 tbsp tamarind paste
4 tbsp coconut nectar or
   honey
1 tbsp groundnut oil
4cm piece of fresh ginger,
   peeled and grated
1 Scotch bonnet chilli,
   deseeded (if preferred) and
   finely chopped
300ml beef stock
salt and cayenne pepper
coriander leaves, to serve
salad, to serve

In a small bowl, combine the coconut sugar or brown sugar, peanut flour, celery salt and onion granules and season with salt and cayenne pepper to taste. Coat the ribs in the rub, cover and leave to marinate in the fridge overnight.

When you are ready to cook the ribs, preheat the oven to 140°C/Gas 1 and transfer them to a large roasting tin with a wire rack. Pour 500ml water into the bottom of the roasting tin, cover tightly in foil and roast for 3 hours, checking halfway through that the water doesn't need topping up. (Alternatively, you could use two smaller tins with racks and fill each with 250ml water – just make sure to place them on the same shelf so they cook evenly.)

Meanwhile, mix the tamarind paste with the coconut nectar or honey, groundnut oil, ginger and Scotch bonnet in a small saucepan. Set the pan over a medium heat and slowly stir in the beef stock. Cook for 10 minutes until reduced and syrupy, then set aside.

After their 3 hours, take the ribs out of the oven and brush with the tamarind sauce. Put them under a hot grill (or 200°C on a fan grill setting) and grill the ribs for 5 minutes. Remove from the grill, turn them over and brush on any additional tamarind sauce. Cook for 5 minutes on the other side, until the glaze turns sticky and crispy in places.

To serve, divide each rack into two, sprinkle with some coriander leaves and enjoy with a salad. Eat hot.

SUYA LAMB CURRY

Goat meat kebabs dusted with suya spice and wrapped in newspaper are a popular street food in Nigeria, as well as other parts of West Africa. They go hand in hand with the summer weather and an ice-cold drink. However, in the UK we're not always gifted with sunshine and can often find ourselves turning to a curry in the colder months. Combining the two together brings the best of both worlds and turns a simple street food into an amazing home dish. Rather than blushing from licking the spice off the newspaper, as I used to do when I was about nine, you'll be blushing from licking the bowl clean. As with most curries, the recipe takes a couple of hours, so it's definitely something I recommend making at the weekend. If you like raw onions, slice a few red onions and serve them on the side. I enjoy eating this with plain boiled rice or Agege Bread (page 152) as both soak up the flavour from the curry making each bite memorable. I've used lamb as it's the closest alternative in terms of taste and is more readily available than goat meat.

PREP TIME: 20 MINS
COOKING TIME: 2 HOURS
  15 MINS
SERVES: 4

1kg lamb leg shank, diced
2 red onions, sliced
4 garlic cloves, sliced
4cm piece of fresh ginger,
  peeled and grated
2 habanero peppers
2 tbsp coconut oil
400ml tin coconut milk
sea salt flakes and white
  pepper
a handful of parsley, to serve

FOR THE SUYA SPICE MIX
3 uda pods, deseeded and
  bark discarded
100g cashew nuts, roasted
  and coarsely ground
½ tsp chilli powder
½ tsp smoked paprika
  powder
1 tsp ground ginger
1 tsp garlic powder
1 tsp onion granules

Preheat the oven to 180°C/Gas 4.

Using a pestle and mortar, grind all the ingredients for the suya spice until you have a fine powder. In a large bowl, season the diced lamb with the suya mix, salt and pepper, and set aside to marinate.

Put the onions, garlic, ginger and habanero peppers in a food processor and blitz to create a paste.

Over a medium heat, melt the coconut oil in a large casserole dish and add the onion paste. Fry for 5 minutes before adding the marinated lamb. Cook for a few minutes until the meat has browned, then pour in the coconut milk and heat until it begins to bubble, stirring every so often.

Cover the dish with a lid and transfer to the preheated oven. Cook for 1 hour and 30 minutes before removing the lid and cooking for a further 30 minutes – this will allow the sauce to reduce. Taste for seasoning and adjust as you see fit.

Serve the curry scattered with parsley leaves.

❀ NOTES

The longer you wait to eat this curry, the better the flavour will be. To reheat it, place in the oven at 180°C/Gas 4 for about 15 minutes, then serve immediately. If you have a slow cooker, you could just put all the ingredients in at once and cook for 2 hours on a high setting.

NIGERIAN-STYLE LAMB PIES

When I used to go to the beach with my family, my uncle would bring an assortment of pies, Scotch eggs, doughnuts and rice for our picnics. My attention was fixed firmly on the pies – they reminded me of Cornish pasties, only spicier. Pies in Nigeria aren't usually made at home – they're picked up from fast-food restaurants or bakeries. In this recipe, I've tried to recreate the flavours of those pies I enjoyed on the beach.

**PREP TIME: 30 MINS
PLUS CHILLING TIME
COOKING TIME: 1 HOUR 10 MINS
SERVES: 4**

FOR THE PASTRY
400g plain flour
50g cassava flour (or use
 a further 50g plain flour)
2 tsp baking powder
1 tsp ground nutmeg
1 tsp ground coriander
1 tsp salt
125g coconut oil, melted
2 large egg yolks, beaten
2 large egg whites beaten
 with 4 tsp water, to glaze

FOR THE LAMB FILLING
1 tbsp groundnut oil
½ onion, finely chopped
½ Scotch bonnet chilli,
 deseeded (if preferred) and
 chopped
2 sprigs of thyme (optional)
1 bay leaf (optional)
250g lamb mince
1 small white-flesh sweet
 potato, finely chopped
½ small carrot, finely chopped
1 tbsp cassava flour or plain
 flour
1 tsp onion granules
1 tsp celery salt
1 tsp ground cloves
½ tsp turmeric
½ tsp ground cumin
salt, white pepper and
 cayenne pepper

Preheat the oven to 180ºC/Gas 4 and line a baking tray with baking paper.

Use a food processor or, if you have the time, your hands to combine the flour, baking powder, nutmeg, coriander, salt, coconut oil and egg yolks until crumbs form. Tip the mix into a large bowl and gradually add up to 125ml ice-cold water, using your hands to form a slightly sticky ball of dough. Note you won't necessarily need to use all the water, so add it slowly until the dough just starts to come together. Wrap the dough in cling film and leave to chill for an hour in the fridge.

Meanwhile, on a medium–high heat, add the groundnut oil to a large frying pan and cook the onion, Scotch bonnet and thyme sprigs and bay leaf, if using, for 5 minutes. Add the lamb mince and fry for roughly 10 minutes, stirring constantly to break it up. Once the mince is well browned, add the sweet potato and carrot, cover and cook for a further 3 minutes. Sprinkle over the flour, onion granules, celery salt, ground cloves, turmeric and cumin. Stir well and add 60ml water. Taste for salt and both peppers before reducing the heat to low. Cover the pan and leave to simmer for 30 minutes, until the gravy has thickened. Allow the lamb mixture to cool before taking the pastry out of the fridge.

Divide the dough into 8 even pieces. One by one, roll each out on a lightly floured surface with a rolling pin to a thickness of about 5mm. Use a small bowl or large pastry cutter to cut 8 circular shapes from the rolled dough that are about 12cm in diameter. Place about 1½ tablespoons of the lamb filling on to the centre of each disc. Brush the edges with the egg-white wash and carefully draw up both sides so they meet at the top, pinching along the spine to seal them together. Lift each pie on to the prepped baking tray and brush with the egg-white wash.

Bake the pies in the oven for 15–20 minutes, until golden. Leave to cool for roughly 5 minutes before serving, or alternatively, enjoy them cold at a picnic.

SPINACH AND LAMB STEW

Efo Riro (Yoruba)

This hearty stew is a popular everyday dish in Yoruba cuisine. It doesn't have too much liquid added as ideally it is a thick and rich and not at all watery, so you want it to reduce as much as possible. It is usually eaten with Egusi Soup (see page 18) and Eba (see page 29), but you could also serve it with plain boiled rice.

PREP TIME: 15 MINS
COOKING TIME: 35 MINS
SERVES: 4

2 red peppers, deseeded and chopped
4 celery sticks, chopped
4 tbsp palm oil or coconut oil
500g diced lamb leg
1 onion, thinly sliced
2 Scotch bonnet chillies, deseeded (if preferred) and chopped
2 tbsp carob powder
½ tsp ground cloves
2 tsp onion granules
1 tsp celery salt
1 tsp ground turmeric
1 tsp dried parsley
800g baby leaf spinach, chopped
salt and cayenne pepper

Use a food processor to purée the peppers and celery sticks, then set aside.

In a large, heavy-based frying pan set over a medium–high heat, melt the palm oil or coconut oil. In two batches, brown the lamb all over for roughly 4 minutes. Remove the lamb from the pan, using a slotted spoon and transfer to a plate.

Reduce the heat to low, add the onion and Scotch bonnet and cook for roughly 10 minutes until soft and translucent. Stir in the puréed vegetables along with the carob powder, cloves, onion granules, celery salt, turmeric and parsley. Bring the heat up to high and let cook for roughly 5 minutes.

Return the lamb to the pan and season to taste with salt and cayenne pepper. Finally, add in the chopped spinach, cover with a lid, bring the heat down to low and simmer for 10 minutes, or until the lamb is cooked through.

Divide the stew between four bowls and serve.

BAOBAB LAMB CUTLETS

I'm a big fan of marinating — it adds such depth and intensity to the flavours you're using. This baobab-based marinade is perfect for lamb and cutlets are super quick to cook, so really there's very little prep time involved — just a little forward planning. Serve with Yam Pottage (see page 38) for a really comforting dinner.

PREP TIME: 10 MINS
COOKING TIME: 25 MINS
SERVES: 4

6 tbsp groundnut oil, plus
    extra for grilling
2 tbsp baobab powder
2 tsp onion granules
1 tsp ground ginger
1 tsp celery salt
1 tsp dried chilli flakes
8 lamb cutlets
crushed peanuts or cashew
    nuts, to serve

FOR THE SPINACH YOGHURT
200g coconut yoghurt or
    Greek yoghurt
75g baby spinach, chopped
1 tsp lemon juice
salt and black pepper

In a bowl, combine the groundnut oil, baobab powder, onion granules, ginger, celery salt and dried chilli flakes. Coat the cutlets with the marinade and cover with cling film. Let marinate in the fridge for 4 hours, or overnight.

Heat a generous drizzle of groundnut oil in a cast-iron grill pan over a medium–high heat and add 4 of the cutlets. Cook the cutlets for 5–6 minutes on each side until browned on the outside. Repeat for the remaining 4 cutlets, adding a little more oil if you need to.

Meanwhile, mix the coconut or Greek yoghurt with the spinach and lemon juice. Season to taste with salt and black pepper.

To serve, plate the cutlets and sprinkle over some crushed nuts. Serve with the spinach yoghurt on the side.

BEEF AND AMALA STEW POT

My family were sceptical about this recipe when I first made it, probably because dried yam flour is usually used to make a type of Okele called amala (see page 28), and not for much else. However, I'm pleased to say that they're firm converts and now love this stew pot. I've used the flour to create soft, pillow-like dumplings, spiced with cloves to get rid of the usually bitter aftertaste. It's quite a hearty dish, so it's perfect for the colder months — that's when we enjoy it most.

PREP TIME: 30 MINS
COOKING TIME: 1 HOUR
SERVES: 4

1 onion, chopped
4cm piece of fresh ginger,
    peeled and chopped
2 celery sticks, chopped
2 tbsp coconut oil
1 Scotch bonnet chilli,
    deseeded (if preferred) and
    finely chopped
400g diced beef
600ml beef stock
200ml rice milk
2 bay leaves
2 uda pods, deseeded and
    bark discarded (optional)
½ medium puna yam or
    8 small white-flesh sweet
    potatoes, peeled and diced
400g tin black-eyed beans,
    drained
100g spinach, chopped
salt and cayenne pepper

FOR THE DUMPLINGS
160g dried yam flour
1 tsp ground cloves
1 tsp salt

To make the dumplings, sift the dried yam flour into a large bowl and add the ground cloves and salt. Using a hand mixer or stand mixer with a dough-hook attachment, combine the flour with 4 tablespoons water, adding a tablespoon at a time, until you have a slightly wet, but not sticky, dough. You do not need to knead the dough, just roll into walnut-sized balls then flatten them into pillow shapes. Cover with cling film and set aside.

Using a blender, purée the onion, ginger and celery along with 60ml water. Place a large saucepan over a medium heat, melt the coconut oil, then pour the blended vegetables into the pan. Let cook for roughly 5 minutes until the colour darkens and some of the excess water has evaporated. Add the chopped Scotch bonnet to the pan along with the diced beef and cook for 10 minutes until the beef has browned all over. Turn the heat up to high, then add the beef stock, rice milk, bay leaves and uda pods, if using. Season with salt and cayenne pepper to taste and bring to the boil, then reduce the heat to low and let simmer, with the lid on, for 20 minutes.

Add the yam and black-eyed beans to the pot and stir in. Replace the lid and cook for a further 15 minutes. Add the spinach to the stew and drop in the yam dumplings. Continue cooking for a further 10 minutes, uncovered, until the yam is cooked and easy to cut through, the beef tears apart easily and the dumplings are cooked and an even colour throughout (cut one in half to check).

Ladle the hot stew into bowls to serve.

MALT BRAISED BEEF

For me, this is the perfect thing to make on a rainy weekend afternoon. Warming and soothing with rich flavours and tender beef, it complements the UK weather particularly well. I've said before that malt is a bit of an acquired taste, but it goes so well with the robust flavours in this dish that I urge you to try it. I love recipes that you can just pull together and leave to do their thing, and this is a classic example.

PREP TIME: 15 MINS
COOKING TIME: 3 HOURS 20 MINS
SERVES: 4

2 tbsp groundnut oil, plus a drizzle if needed
4 thick cuts beef shin (about 800g in total), bone in
2 tbsp rice flour, for dusting
1 tbsp ground nutmeg, for dusting
1 large onion, halved and thinly sliced
2 celery sticks, chopped
2 tbsp malt extract
300g mushrooms, chopped
1 beef stock cube
4 sprigs of thyme
2 bay leaves
2 tsp onion granules
1 tsp celery salt
½ tsp ground cloves
1 tsp ground nutmeg
salt
Onion Millet (page 60), to serve (optional)

Preheat the oven to 180°C/Gas 4.

Cover the bottom of a large casserole dish with the groundnut oil and set over a medium–high heat. Put the beef in a large bowl, sprinkle over the rice flour and nutmeg, and mix until well coated. Sear the beef for 3–4 minutes on each side until well browned, then set aside on a plate. Reduce the heat to medium and add the onion and celery to the pan, with a little more oil if needed, and cook for 5 minutes until the onion is softened.

In a large measuring jug, mix 800ml boiling water with the malt extract and beef stock cube. Add a few tablespoons of the malt stock to the casserole dish to lift any vegetables from the base. Put the beef back into the casserole dish along with the chopped mushrooms, thyme and bay leaves. Pour in the rest of the malt stock and season with the onion granules, celery salt, spices and salt. Turn the heat up to high and bring the stock almost to a boil, then cover with a lid and transfer to the oven. Cook for 3 hours, basting the meat occasionally with the juices and adding up to 200ml extra water if you think the sauce is reducing too much.

Once the beef is tender, carefully remove the casserole dish from the oven and allow to cool for 5 minutes. Transfer the meat to plates or bowls and ladle the sauce over the top. Serve warm with onion millet, rice or mashed potatoes.

SUYA BEEF BURGERS

When I was younger, what I looked forward to most were the weekends when we'd travel as a family to Abeokuta, a large city in southwest Nigeria, to eat street food. My favourite dish of all was suya, and my cousins and I would have competitions to see who could eat the most without drinking any water. I never lost. In fact, I would usually lick off the leftover spices from the wrapper. Many years later, when I was at university, the only thing that would excite me as much as suya did back then was, and possibly still is, a juicy beef burger after a night out! Unlike the Suya Lamb Curry (see page 132), this burger is much faster to make and much more similar to traditional street food. It doesn't require lots of toppings because the flavour is all in the patty and it reminds me of those finger-licking days in Abeokuta.

PREP TIME: 15 MINS
COOKING TIME: 20 MINS
SERVES: 4

2 tbsp groundnut oil
1 red onion, finely chopped
4cm piece of fresh ginger,
  peeled and finely grated
seeds from 2 uda pods,
  crushed (optional)
500g beef or lamb mince
  (20% fat)
1 tbsp roasted peanut flour or
  2 tbsp crushed peanuts
2 tsp onion granules
1 tsp ground ginger
2 tsp cayenne pepper
  (optional)
1 tsp salt

TO ASSEMBLE
4–8 Agege Bread slices or
  4 agege rolls (see notes)
4 tbsp peanut butter or
  cashew butter
baby leaf spinach
½ red onion, thinly sliced
2 salad tomatoes, sliced

Heat 1 tablespoon of the groundnut oil in a small frying pan over a medium heat. Add the onion and ginger along with the crushed uda seeds, if using, and cook for 4 minutes until the onion is softened. Transfer to a large bowl and add the mince, peanut flour or peanuts, onion granules, ginger, cayenne pepper, if using, and salt. Use your hands to mix everything together until well combined and the spices appear evenly distributed throughout the mixture.

Divide the meat equally into 4 portions and shape each into a round flat disc. Heat the remaining tablespoon of groundnut oil in a griddle pan over a medium heat, and grill the patties for 4–6 minutes on each side, depending on how well done you like your meat.

Lightly toast the bread slices and place each patty on a slice of the bread. Top with a spoonful of peanut butter, baby leaf spinach, sliced onion and sliced tomatoes. Finish with another slice of bread (if using).

❁ NOTES

If you have the time, you could make proper agege rolls using the braided Agege Bread recipe (see page 152). After the second prove, divide the dough pieces into 8 and shape each one into a ball, then flatten slightly. Bake the rolls for roughly 10 minutes until risen and browned and keep the remaining 4 for later use. You could use brioche buns in place of agege, if they are easier to find.

MORINGA AND BEEF STEW WITH BEAN DUMPLINGS

Miyan Zogale da Danwake (Hausa)

Here I've combined two traditional Hausa dishes to make a really hearty casserole. Miyan Zogale translates as moringa soup and is often eaten in northern Nigeria. Danwake is a dumpling made from bean flour and baobab leaves. While you might recognize moringa and baobab as superfoods that can be found in health-food stores, in Nigeria they're simply considered fruit and leaves and are easily found in markets across the northern parts of the country. These ingredients add a nice nutritional boost to this hybrid dish. In place of the bean flour, cornmeal can be used, as traditionally Miyan Zogale is served with a fufu-style dish known as tuwo masara. If you'd like to have the stew without dumplings, feel free to eat it with millet instead.

PREP TIME: 20 MINS
COOKING TIME: 2 HOURS
SERVES: 4

2 tsp celery salt
4 tsp onion granules
800g braising beef
4 tbsp coconut oil
1 white onion, halved and
  sliced
4 salad tomatoes, halved and
  sliced
120g peanut butter or
  cashew butter
600ml beef stock
2 tsp carob powder
2 tbsp moringa powder
salt and cayenne pepper

FOR THE DUMPLINGS
200g bean flour
2 tbsp baobab powder
1 tsp baking powder
1 beef stock cube, crushed

Preheat the oven to 180°C/Gas 4.

Combine the celery salt and onion granules and rub all over the beef. Melt the coconut oil in a large casserole dish over a high heat and sear the meat for 10 minutes until browned. You will need to do this in batches so that you don't overcrowd the pan. Remove the meat from the casserole dish with a slotted spoon and set aside on a plate.

Reduce the heat to medium, add the onion and tomatoes to the pan and fry for 5 minutes until slightly soft, then add the peanut butter or cashew butter and cook for a further 5 minutes. Return the beef to the casserole dish and add the stock, carob powder and moringa powder. Bring the heat up to medium–high and let cook for 15 minutes, stirring, until the stew starts to thicken. Season with salt before covering with a lid and placing in the preheated oven for 1 hour.

Meanwhile, sift the bean flour, baobab powder, baking powder and crushed stock cube into a bowl and season with cayenne pepper and salt. Add about 180ml cold water to the flour mix to form a soft and slightly sticky dough – you may need to add up to 2 tablespoons more water to make it come together, but add it slowly. Wet your hands and roll tablespoon-scoops of the bean dough into balls.

Once the beef has been in the oven for an hour, uncover and place the dumpling balls on top. Replace the lid and cook for a final 20 minutes. The dumplings should be swollen.

To serve, scoop the stew and dumplings into bowls. Best enjoyed when you are wrapped up in a few layers during the winter months.

STACKED SHANGO BEEF STEAKS

I really wanted to create a dish inspired by Nigerian culture, specifically Yoruba folklore, to include in this book. These steaks really make me think of the Yoruba god of fire (Orisha), Shango, because they are fiery red in colour. Coconut oil can be used instead of palm oil, but it won't quite be the same. They're very quick to cook because of the cut, but there's no reason you can't replace the minute steaks with four thicker steaks — just make sure to adjust the cooking times accordingly. These are best eaten with some sweet-potato chips and a glass of milk.

PREP TIME: 10 MINS
COOKING TIME: 10 MINS
SERVES: 4

3 tbsp palm oil
12 beef minute steaks

FOR THE 'BUTTER'
1 tbsp coconut aminos or
   1tsp shrimp paste
2 tbsp palm vinegar or white
   wine vinegar
2cm piece of fresh ginger,
   peeled and grated
½ garlic clove, finely diced
¼ onion, finely diced
1 tbsp chopped parsley
4 tbsp coconut oil

FOR THE RUB
2 uda pods, deseeded and
   bark discarded
1 tbsp cayenne pepper
1 tsp coarsely ground black
   pepper

Pour the coconut aminos or shrimp paste and palm vinegar or wine vinegar into a saucepan and stir in the ginger, garlic and onion. Cook over a medium heat until the onion and garlic begin to soften. Remove from the pan and transfer to a bowl. Add the chopped parsley and the coconut oil, mixing until everything is combined. Cover the bowl with cling film and leave to cool in the fridge.

To make the rub, grind the uda seeds, cayenne pepper and black pepper together in a pestle and mortar. Using the same pan as before, heat the palm oil while you rub the pepper mix into the steaks, making sure to coat both sides. Flash fry the steaks over a high heat for 1 minute on each side, or however you prefer them cooked. You will probably need to do this in batches.

To serve, layer 3 steaks on top of each other, making sure to sandwich a tablespoon of the aminos 'butter' between each and on top of the last.

SEARED VENISON IN UDA SAUCE

I'm a big fan of venison and although it's not really used in Nigerian culture, the taste goes extremely well with Nigerian flavours. This was one of my successful experiments after trying to imitate a peppercorn sauce using uda instead. Uda has a woody scent with a hint of lemon but tastes sweet when cooked in creamy sauces, making this very moreish.

PREP TIME: 10 MINS
COOKING TIME: 25 MINS
SERVES: 4

4 venison steaks
2 tbsp groundnut oil
salt and black pepper

FOR THE UDA SAUCE
1 tbsp coconut oil
1 small white onion, minced
4cm piece of fresh ginger, minced
2 tbsp coconut aminos
3 uda pods, crushed
1 tsp black pepper
1 tsp white pepper
1 tsp onion granules
1 bay leaf
160ml coconut cream
2 tsp freshly squeezed lemon juice
cayenne pepper

Season the venison with salt and pepper and set aside.

To make the sauce, melt the coconut oil in a large frying pan over a medium heat. Add the onion and ginger and cook for 7 minutes, stirring occasionally, until the onion is cooked and softened. Turn the heat down to low and add the coconut aminos to the pan. Add the crushed uda pods, peppers, onion granules, bay leaf and 80ml water, and leave to simmer for 5 minutes. Remove the bay leaf and uda pods, then mix in the coconut cream and lemon juice. Add salt and cayenne pepper to taste. Put the sauce in a small bowl and set aside.

Rinse the pan and pat dry with kitchen paper. Turn up the heat to high and add the groundnut oil. When the oil is hot, add the venison and sear for 5 minutes on each side. Remove from the pan and place on a chopping board to cool slightly. When the venison is cool enough to handle, slice each steak into strips.

Distribute the sauce evenly among plates and top with the sliced venison. Serve hot!

Baking and Desserts

BRAIDED AGEGE BREAD

Agege bread is the most popular type of bread in Nigeria. It's a very soft, sweet bread and is usually accompanied by Bell Pepper Soup (Obe Ata – see page 17), scrambled eggs or stewed beans. It tastes quite similar to brioche, although its texture is a lot softer. Nigerians don't tend to use milk when making bread, primarily because dairy doesn't play a major role in Nigerian diets. Eggs aren't used either, although I've never known why this is the case. What I do know is that agege bread is delicious and versatile – you can make it into any shape you wish.

PREP TIME: 45 MINS PLUS PROVING AND COOLING TIME
COOKING TIME: 25 MINS
MAKES: 2 LOAVES

330g plain flour, plus extra for dusting
1 tsp ground nutmeg
1 tbsp caster sugar
1 tsp salt
¾ tsp fast-action dried yeast
2 tbsp coconut oil, softened (not melted), plus extra for greasing
1 egg white mixed with 1 tsp water, for glazing

FOR THE CASSAVA PASTE
2 tbsp caster sugar
1 tbsp cassava flour or plain flour
½ tsp pineapple essence
1 tbsp coconut oil

To make the cassava paste, combine the sugar and cassava flour in a small saucepan. While mixing, slowly add 125ml water and the pineapple essence to form a milk-like liquid. Set the pan over a high heat and whisk until it thickens to a wet paste. Take off the heat and stir in the coconut oil until it's fully melted, then leave to cool.

Put the plain flour in a large bowl and add the nutmeg, sugar and salt on one side and the yeast on the other. Create a well in the centre and slowly add in the cassava paste, plus an extra 125ml warm water, mixing until all the ingredients start to stick together to form a dough

Put the dough on a lightly floured surface and knead using a floured rolling pin. The idea here is to flatten the dough out, squeeze it back together, flip and repeat for 10 minutes until it becomes elastic. You may need to re-flour the surface as you go.

Slowly add the coconut oil, a tablespoon at a time, kneading for a further 10 minutes. The dough is ready when it doesn't stick to the rolling pin, at which point, place it in a large bowl that has been greased with a little coconut oil and cover with cling film. Leave to prove for an hour, or until the dough doubles in size. Grease two 1lb loaf tins with coconut oil.

Lightly flour your surface again, tip out the dough and knock it back with your fist to remove any air. Squeeze the dough and shape into a ball before cutting into 6 equal pieces. Take 3 pieces and roll each one into a sausage 25cm long. Braid the strands together, not too tightly, so it can expand when baking. Pinch the ends together and then tuck underneath to form a neat plait. Repeat with the remaining 3 pieces of dough to make another loaf. Transfer the braids into the prepared loaf tins and leave to prove for another hour in a warm area. As it gets towards the end of the proving time, preheat the oven to 200ºC/Gas 6.

When the bread is ready to be baked, brush the tops lightly with some of the egg wash. Bake for 20 minutes until well browned. Remove the agege from the tins and place on a cooling rack for at least 10 minutes. Serve warm.

PUFF PUFF

Other than the traditional clothing and vibrant music, one thing I really looked forward to at Nigerian weddings was the Puff Puff. Puff Puff is a Nigerian-style doughnut and, I imagine, gets its name from how it puffs up when deep-fried. Most Nigerian weddings tend to serve the food buffet style and I would pile these treats on to my plate before finding somewhere quiet to enjoy them – photographers always seemed to like capturing the guests mid-bite, with mouths wide open.

The trick to making perfect Puff Puff is to make sure it's deep-fried for the right amount of time – too long and you'll have an unpleasant taste and greasy lips, too little and you won't achieve an all-over crispy brown coat. The right balance of flour and a well-moderated oil heat are also essential. Puff Puff is generally only ever made using one method, but there are endless possible accompaniments, some of which I've provided here.

BASIC PUFF PUFF

PREP TIME: 20 MINS, PLUS PROVING TIME
COOKING TIME: 30 MINS
MAKES: 12–16

480g plain flour, plus extra for dusting
100g golden caster sugar
1 tsp ground nutmeg
2 tsp fast-action dried yeast
340ml rice milk or almond milk, warmed
1 tsp vanilla extract
groundnut oil, for frying

Sift the flour into a large bowl and add the sugar, nutmeg and yeast. Create a well in the centre of the bowl and add the rice milk and vanilla extract. Using a hand mixer, with a dough-hook attachment, mix the batter until well incorporated – the dough should look almost like a thick pancake batter. Let the dough sit, covered with a tea towel and in a warm place, for about 30 minutes, or until slightly thickened.

Line a colander with kitchen paper, then fill a medium saucepan with oil, two-thirds of the way full, and place over a medium–high heat. To test that the oil is hot enough, drop a teaspoonful of the batter into the oil and it should sizzle and rise to the top almost straight away.

Dust your hands with flour, scoop an ice-cream scoopful of the batter and roll it into a ball between your palms. Repeat to make 4 balls, then carefully drop them into the hot oil. The balls should sink then rise straight to the top. It's important to not overcrowd the pan, so only fry 4 balls at a time. After roughly 3 minutes, once the balls of puff puff are floating at the top of the oil and you notice the sides under the oil start to brown up, flip the balls over and cook for a further 3 minutes. While they are cooking, continue scooping and rolling the next batch.

Use a slotted spoon to take the balls of puff puff out of the oil and transfer to the lined colander. Let drain and cool down for a few minutes. Continue until all the dough is used up. Serve warm.

CHOCOLATE CHILLI PUFF PUFF

**PREP TIME: 45 MINS, PLUS
 PROVING TIME
COOKING TIME: 35 MINS
MAKES: 12–16**

420g plain flour, plus extra
 for dusting
60g cocoa powder
3 tsp cayenne pepper
 (optional)
100g golden caster sugar
4 tsp fast-action dried yeast
340ml rice milk or almond
 milk, warmed
groundnut oil, for frying
400ml Ogi (page 173) or
 custard
200g dark chocolate
1 tsp vanilla extract
icing sugar, for dusting
hot chocolate, to serve
 (optional)

Sift the flour and cocoa powder into a large bowl and add 2 teaspoons of the cayenne pepper, if using, along with the sugar and yeast. Create a well in the centre of the bowl and add the rice milk. Using a hand mixer, with a dough-hook attachment, mix the batter until well incorporated – the dough should look almost like a thick pancake batter. Let the dough sit, covered with a tea towel and in a warm place, for about 30 minutes, or until slightly thickened.

Line a colander with kitchen paper, then fill a saucepan with oil, two-thirds of the way full, and place over a medium–high heat. To test that the oil is hot enough, drop a teaspoonful of the batter into the oil and it should sizzle and rise to the top almost straight away.

Dust your hands with flour, scoop an ice-cream scoopful of the batter and roll it into a ball between your palms. Repeat to make 4 balls, then carefully drop them into the hot oil. The balls should sink then rise straight to the top. It's important to not overcrowd the pan, so only fry 4 balls at a time. After roughly 3 minutes, once the balls of puff puff are floating at the top of the oil and you notice the sides under the oil start to brown up, flip the balls over and cook for a further 3 minutes. While they are cooking, continue scooping and rolling the next batch.

Use a slotted spoon to take the balls of puff puff out of the oil and transfer to the lined colander. Let drain and cool down for a few minutes. Continue until all the dough is used up.

While the puff puff cools, put the ogi and the dark chocolate into a pan set over a medium heat, stirring gently. Once the chocolate is fully melted and combined with the ogi, stir in the vanilla extract and the remaining teaspoon of cayenne pepper, if using.

Transfer the filling to a piping bag. Make a hole in each puff puff using a skewer then fill with the chocolate chilli ogi. Be careful not to overfill. Dust lightly with icing sugar and serve warm with a mug of hot chocolate, if you like.

HIBISCUS DRIZZLE PUFF PUFF

PREP TIME: 25 MINS, PLUS PROVING TIME
COOKING TIME: 45 MINS
MAKES: 12–16

480g plain flour, plus extra
    for dusting
150g golden caster sugar
3 tbsp fine-cut dried hibiscus
    flowers
1 tsp ground nutmeg
2 tsp fast-action dried yeast
340ml rice milk or almond
    milk, warmed
1 tsp vanilla extract
groundnut oil, for frying
moringa tea or any herbal
    green tea, to serve
    (optional)

Sift the flour into a large bowl and add 100g of the sugar, 1 tablespoon of the hibiscus, the nutmeg and the yeast. Create a well in the centre of the bowl and add the rice milk and vanilla extract. Using a hand mixer, with a dough-hook attachment, mix the batter until well incorporated – the dough should look almost like a thick pancake batter. Let the dough sit, covered with a tea towel and in a warm place, for about 30 minutes, or until slightly thickened.

Line a colander with kitchen paper, then fill a medium saucepan with oil, two-thirds of the way full, and place over a medium–high heat. To test that the oil is hot enough, drop a teaspoonful of the batter into the oil and it should sizzle and rise to the top almost straight away.

Dust your hands with flour, scoop an ice-cream scoopful of the batter and roll it into a ball between your palms. Repeat to make 4 balls, then carefully drop them into the hot oil. The balls should sink then rise straight to the top. It's important to not overcrowd the pan, so only fry 4 balls at a time. After roughly 3 minutes, once the balls of puff puff are floating at the top of the oil and you notice the sides under the oil start to brown up, flip the balls over and cook for a further 3 minutes. While they are cooking, continue scooping and rolling the next batch.

Use a slotted spoon to take the balls of puff puff out of the oil and transfer to the lined colander. Let drain and cool down for a few minutes. Continue until all the dough is used up.

While the puff puff cools, put 1 tablespoon of the hibiscus petals, the remaining caster sugar and 100ml water in a small saucepan. Gently heat over a medium–low heat until the sugar dissolves and the water turns purple. Cook for about 15 minutes until the syrup thickens, then leave to cool.

Pierce a few small holes into the puff puff and then drizzle over the sweetened hibiscus syrup. Let soak for 5 minutes before sprinkling on the remaining tablespoon of hibiscus petals. Serve warm with moringa tea, if you like.

❀ NOTES
To keep the puff puff warm before serving, preheat the oven to a very low heat before you start frying. Once they've been blotted on kitchen paper, put them on a baking tray and in the oven. The puff puff may end up with tiny 'legs', depending on how fast you work, but it's nothing to worry about. I also think it adds a bit of character.

ABIGAIL'S SPICY BANANA BREAD

I have quite a sweet tooth, so when I was first introduced to the idea of a spicy banana cake, I protested. However, after tasting it, I was a convert. This recipe was introduced to me by my good friend Abigail. The bread has the perfect balance of spices to complement the sweetness of the banana.

**PREP TIME: 15 MINS
    PLUS COOLING TIME
COOKING TIME: 45 MINS
MAKES: 1 LOAF**

100g coconut oil, softened
    (not melted), plus extra for
    greasing
175g coconut sugar or
    demerara sugar
2 large eggs
1 tsp vanilla extract
220g plain flour
1 tsp bicarbonate of soda
5 tbsp rice milk (or any
    alternative nut milk)
1 tsp ground nutmeg
1 tsp coarsely ground black
    pepper
1 tsp crushed chilli flakes
3 ripe bananas, mashed

Preheat the oven to 180°C/Gas 4 and grease a 1lb loaf tin with coconut oil.

In a large mixing bowl, cream together the softened coconut oil and sugar. One at a time, beat in the eggs, then add the vanilla extract and beat until everything is well incorporated. Sift in the flour and bicarbonate of soda, and fold in. At this point your batter will be really thick, so add in your milk and mix some more. Finally, fold in your spices and the mashed bananas.

Pour the mixture into the prepared loaf tin and bake in the preheated oven for 45 minutes. To test whether the banana bread is cooked, an inserted skewer or knife should come out clean.

Allow the banana bread to cool in the tin for 10 minutes before transferring to a cooling rack.

✿ NOTES

If your bananas aren't ripe, place them in an oven (preheated to 140°C/Gas 1) for about 15 minutes before setting them aside to cool.

GARRI AND CACAO BARS

In Nigeria, after spending the weekend with my family, I would return to boarding school with bags of garri and tins of powdered chocolate and powdered milk, provided by my grandma. Sweets and other treats weren't allowed in the dormitories, so I had to carefully plan my arrival to avoid running into house mother or any prefects. The girls I shared my room with taught me how to make chocolate 'bars' by sandwiching the powdered milk and chocolate between two sheets of paper and using the tins to roll and compress them. The bars were then sprinkled with garri and enjoyed by everyone in the room. This recipe is an enhanced no-bake version of those chocolate bars.

**PREP TIME: 15 MINS
PLUS COOLING TIME
COOKING TIME: 10 MINS
MAKES: 21 BARS**

150g garri
100g rolled oats
75g egusi seeds or flaked almonds
60g coconut oil
120g coconut nectar or honey
60g soft light brown sugar
¼ tsp vanilla or almond extract
200g chocolate chips

Line a 20cm square baking tin with baking paper, making sure there is some hanging over each edge.

In a large bowl, combine the garri, oats and egusi seeds and stir with a large wooden spoon until well combined. Put the coconut oil, coconut nectar or honey, sugar and vanilla or almond extract in a saucepan and set over a medium heat, stirring occasionally, until the coconut oil is melted and the sugar is completely dissolved. Add the syrup to the dry ingredients and mix until well combined. Spoon the mixture into the prepared tin and use a rubber spatula to firmly press it into the tin. Let sit for roughly 5 minutes.

Meanwhile, put the chocolate chips in a glass bowl and set it over a pan of simmering water, being careful that the bottom of the bowl doesn't touch the water. Melt the chocolate, stirring occasionally until smooth. Pour the melted chocolate over the garri mix in the tin and spread it out evenly using a rubber spatula or the back of a spoon. Let cool for 10–15 minutes, before placing in the fridge to chill for a further 2 hours.

Once the chocolate has hardened, use the baking paper to lift the traybake out of the tin. Using a sharp knife, cut it into 7 slices in one direction, and then 3 in the other to make 21 bars. Store any leftovers in an airtight container.

PEANUT AND TOFFEE BARS

The two most popular snacks at the tuckshop in my boarding school were peanut bars and toffee sticks. Girls, myself included, would unwrap the peanut bars and tightly coil the toffee sticks around them. You were considered a connoisseur if you could wrap the toffee around the bar without leaving any gaps in between. The pair were an infamous duo throughout school because it was one of the few sweet treats we could easily get our hands on. Even now, I still remember how surprisingly soft the bars were, which is why I wanted to recreate this delight.

**PREP TIME: 5 MINS
    PLUS COOLING TIME
COOKING TIME: 20 MINS
MAKES: 18 BARS**

450g caster sugar
1 tbsp coconut oil
½ tsp vanilla extract
300g peanuts

FOR THE TOFFEE WRAP
2 tbsp coconut oil
2 x 397g tins sweetened
    condensed milk
1 tsp vanilla extract

Line a 20cm square baking tin with baking paper.

Over a medium heat, melt the 2 tablespoons of coconut oil for the toffee in a saucepan. Pour in the condensed milk along with the vanilla extract and continuously stir. The milk should start getting thicker and after about 6 minutes will combine to form one light brown mass.

Transfer the toffee to the lined tin and use the back of a spoon to press it down. You might need to use a knife to spread it into the corners of the tin. Set aside and allow to cool.

Put the sugar and 125ml water into a large saucepan set over a medium heat. Stir until well combined and let the sugar dissolve so that there are no visible crystals. Bring the heat up to high and let it boil for about 8 minutes, or until it thickens to a deep amber caramel. Take the pan off the heat and stir in the coconut oil and vanilla extract. Once fully incorporated, add the peanuts to the pan and mix until they are well coated.

Pour the peanut mix over the toffee and use a rubber spatula to spread the mix out into an even, flat layer, making sure to get into all the corners. Cover with another sheet of baking paper and, using a small rolling pin or a bottle, press the peanuts down into the toffee. When you're satisfied, remove the top layer of baking paper (some peanuts will come off) and let cool for 1 hour.

When cooled, take the toffee out of the square tin and pull away the bottom layer of baking paper. Slice into 6 long strips, then cut each strip into 3 bars.

CHIN CHIN

This is a beloved Nigerian treat and, like with so many popular recipes, there are many variations. Some people prefer their Chin Chin to be dough-like and deep-fried. Some people like it almost jaw-breakingly hard, and I suspect this may be where its name derives from. For me, this slightly crunchier version is best – I like it somewhere between a shortbread and a biscotti biscuit. Nigerians also tend to play around with the shape and size of their Chin Chin too. This recipe is quick to make and really delivers on texture and flavour. And you won't lose any teeth in the process. I've provided a traditional version along with two of my favourite flavour variations.

TRADITIONAL CHIN CHIN

**PREP TIME: 20 MINS
   PLUS CHILLING TIME
COOKING TIME: 15–20 MINS
SERVES: 4-6**

300g plain flour, plus extra
   for dusting
½ tsp baking powder
90g caster sugar
1 tsp ground nutmeg
4 tbsp coconut oil, melted
120ml evaporated milk
1 egg
groundnut oil, for deep frying

First line a baking tray with baking paper.

In a large bowl, sift together the flour and baking powder, then add the sugar along with the nutmeg and mix. In a separate bowl, combine the coconut oil, evaporated milk and egg and gently whisk until well combined. Using your hands, combine the wet mix with the dry mix until a smooth dough is formed.

Put the dough on a lightly floured surface and gently roll it out to 3mm thick. Cut into 1cm cubes using a knife and transfer the chin chin to the lined baking tray. Cover with cling film and chill in the refrigerator for 15 minutes.

Half fill a large pan with oil and place it over a medium–high heat. It is hot enough when a piece of the dough sizzles when dropped into the oil. In batches, fry the chin chin in the oil stirring constantly for 2 minutes until golden brown. Use a slotted spoon to remove the chin chin to a wire rack lined with kitchen paper. Repeat to use up all the dough – you may need to do up to 6 batches.

Let cool for 5–10 minutes before eating.

COFFEE CHIN CHIN

**PREP TIME: 20 MINS
PLUS CHILLING TIME
COOKING TIME: 15 MINS
MAKES: 16**

1 tbsp instant coffee granules
300g plain flour, plus extra
  for dusting
½ tsp baking powder
90g demerara sugar
1 tsp ground nutmeg
4 tbsp coconut oil, melted
120ml evaporated milk
1 egg
1 tbsp ground cinnamon
4 tbsp caster sugar

First line a baking tray with baking paper. Dissolve the coffee powder in 1 tablespoon boiling water.

In a large bowl, sift together the flour and baking powder, then add the demerara sugar along with the nutmeg and mix. In a separate bowl, combine the coconut oil, evaporated milk, egg and dissolved coffee powder and gently whisk until well combined. Using your hands, combine the wet mix with the dry mix until a smooth dough is formed.

Put the dough on a lightly floured surface and gently roll it out to 3mm thick. Cut into circles using a 7cm biscuit cutter and transfer the chin chin to the lined baking tray. Cover with cling film and chill in the refrigerator for 15 minutes.

Preheat the oven to 180°C/Gas 4. In a small bowl mix together the cinnamon and caster sugar. Take the chin chin out of the fridge, remove the cling film and sprinkle the cinnamon sugar over each circle. Bake in the oven for 12–15 minutes until golden brown.

Let cool on a wire rack for 10 minutes before serving.

LEMON CHIN CHIN

**PREP TIME: 20 MINS
PLUS CHILLING TIME
COOKING TIME: 15 MINS
MAKES: 36**

300g plain flour, plus extra
for dusting
½ tsp baking powder
4 tbsp caster sugar
zest of 1 lemon
1 tsp ground nutmeg
3 tbsp coconut oil, melted
120ml evaporated milk
1 egg
1 tsp vanilla extract

First line a baking tray with baking paper.

In a large bowl, sift together the flour and baking powder, then add the sugar along with the lemon zest and nutmeg and mix. In a separate bowl, combine the coconut oil, evaporated milk, egg and vanilla extract and gently whisk until well combined. Using your hands, combine the wet mix with the dry mix until a smooth dough is formed.

Put the dough on a lightly floured surface and gently roll it out to 3mm thick. Cut out circles using a 9cm biscuit cutter, then cut each circle into 6 wedges using a knife. If you don't have a cutter, try cutting the biscuits into 3cm squares.

Transfer the chin chin to the lined baking tray. Cover with cling film and chill in the refrigerator for 15 minutes.

Preheat the oven to 180°C/Gas 4. Take the chin chin out of the fridge and remove the cling film. Bake in the oven for 12–15 minutes until golden brown.

Let cool on a wire rack for 10 minutes before serving.

AMALA CHOCOLATE MUFFINS

Yam flour wasn't my favourite growing up but I now realize that this was because I had no idea how versatile it is. I've since discovered that it's one of the few Nigerian flours that can replace plain flour in the same ratios. It changes colour from off-white to mink-brown when cooked, and enhances the colour of the your bake. Plus, it also complements the taste of chocolate perfectly, so I recommend giving it a try – perhaps you'll be a convert, too.

PREP TIME: 20 MINS
COOKING TIME: 18 MINS
MAKES: 12 MUFFINS

120g dried yam flour
100g plain flour
1 tsp ground cloves
1 tsp baking powder
1 tsp bicarbonate of soda
120ml groundnut oil, plus
  extra for greasing
120g caster sugar
1 tsp vanilla extract
2 large eggs
60g cocoa powder
90g coconut sugar
40g chocolate chips

Preheat the oven to 180°C/Gas 4 and line a 12-hole muffin tin with paper cases. Fill and boil a kettle.

In a large bowl, sift together the yam flour, plain flour, ground cloves, baking powder and bicarbonate of soda.

In a smaller bowl, whisk together the groundnut oil, caster sugar, vanilla extract and eggs.

In a second small bowl, mix together the cocoa powder and coconut sugar. Carefully, pour in 250ml boiling water and stir until well combined, then set aside.

Add the egg and oil mixture to the flour and, using an electric hand mixer or stand mixer, beat until well incorporated. The mixture will resemble a wet biscuit mix at this point. Slowly add in the liquefied cocoa, mixing between pours, until it's all been added. You should be left with a thick, chocolatey batter. Fold in the chocolate chips and get ready to spoon into the lined tin.

Use an ice-cream scoop to spoon equal portions of chocolate batter into the paper cases. Transfer the muffin tin to the middle rack of the oven and bake for roughly 18 minutes, or until an inserted knife comes out clean.

Once they're ready, transfer the muffins to a cooling rack and let rest for at least 10 minutes before eating.

KULI KULI

These are a crunchy, savoury treat that hail from the northern parts of Nigeria. Like most Nigerian treats, these are deep fried but I prefer to make them crispy by finishing them in the oven. The key to making good Kuli Kuli is to extract as much oil out of the ground peanuts, just before it becomes a paste, using a nut bag. I've skipped this stage by using roasted peanut flour instead.

PREP TIME: 15 MINS
COOKING TIME: 20 MINS
MAKES: 8–10

160g roasted peanut flour
1 tbsp ground ginger
180ml rice milk
½ tsp almond extract
salt and cayenne pepper
groundnut oil, for shaping
 and frying
vanilla ice cream, to serve

Preheat the oven to 180ºC/Gas 4 and line a baking tray with baking paper.

In a large bowl, mix the peanut flour and ginger together. In a separate bowl, whisk together the rice milk and almond extract. Pour the wet ingredients into the dry ingredients and season to taste with salt and cayenne pepper. Using your hands, mix everything together to form a dough. Coat your hands in groundnut oil and shape the dough into balls about the size of a walnut.

Fill a medium saucepan with groundnut oil to about 3cm deep, and place over a medium–high heat. Carefully drop 4 or 5 balls into the oil and fry for 2 minutes. As the bottoms begin to crisp, turn over and fry for a further 2 minutes. Using a slotted spoon, fish the balls from the oil and place them on the lined baking tray. Repeat with the second batch, then transfer to the oven and bake for 6–8 minutes, until the outsides are crisp but they are still soft and crumbly in the middle when pressed gently. Leave to cool for 5 minutes before serving.

This treat goes down well with vanilla ice cream.

HIBISCUS AND COCONUT CAKE

Hibiscus is a really flavourful ingredient and is very fragrant when cooked, which makes it great for experimenting with. Rather than using almonds for the base of this cake, I've gone for egusi seeds, which are eaten much more regularly in Nigerian culture. Although it doesn't happen often, when I do have time to make cakes, I try to create a real showstopper to share with friends, and this is no exception. Although hibiscus can be eaten all year round, I do think of this as a summer cake to enjoy in the garden.

PREP TIME: 30 MINS
COOKING TIME: 30 MINS
SERVES: 12

180g plain flour
60g ground egusi seeds or
   ground almonds
80g fine-cut dried hibiscus
   petals
1 tsp ground cloves
1 tsp baking powder
1 tsp bicarbonate of soda
½ tsp salt
90g coconut oil, softened
60ml groundnut oil, plus extra
   for greasing
100g caster sugar
80g light brown sugar
3 large eggs
½ x 400ml tin coconut milk
2 tsp vanilla extract
2 tbsp freshly squeezed lemon
   juice
desiccated coconut, to decorate
hibiscus petals, to decorate

FOR THE COCONUT DRIZZLE
120g icing sugar
4 tbsp coconut milk
½ tsp coconut extract
½ tsp vanilla extract

FOR THE COCONUT FROSTING
300g cream cheese
2 tbsp coconut milk
80g icing sugar
1 tbsp fine-cut dried hibiscus
   petals

Preheat the oven to 180°C/Gas 4. Grease two round 20cm cake tins then line them with baking paper.

In a large bowl, mix together the flour, ground egusi seeds or ground almonds, hibiscus petals, ground cloves, baking powder and bicarbonate of soda and salt.

In another large bowl, cream the coconut oil, groundnut oil and sugars together. One by one, add the eggs until well combined. Add half of the dry ingredients to the bowl, followed by half of the coconut milk and mix with an electric hand whisk or stand mixer until well combined, scraping down the sides of the bowl as needed. Repeat to add the remaining dry ingredients and coconut milk and mix to thoroughly combine. Finally, add the vanilla extract and lemon juice, folding in gently.

Transfer the batter into a large measuring jug and evenly distribute it between the two cake tins. If you prefer less washing up, then roughly measure by eye. Bake the cakes for about 30 minutes. When they're ready, a skewer inserted into the centre of the cakes should come out clean. Remove from the oven and leave to cool in the tins for 10 minutes, then turn the cakes out of the tins on to a cooling rack and allow to cool completely.

To make the drizzle, mix the icing sugar with the coconut milk to get a thick drizzle, then add the coconut and vanilla extracts. Trickle over both layers of the cooled hibiscus cake.

For the frosting, whisk all the ingredients together to create a fluffy purple cloud. Make sure the colour is consistent throughout. Spread half the frosting over one of the cakes and place the second on top. Spread what's left of the frosting over the top layer and sprinkle over the desiccated coconut and hibiscus petals to decorate.

CHEAT'S OGI

Ogi, also known as akamu in Igbo, is a custard made from fermented corn kernels – most commonly hominy corn, but yellow corn works equally as well. The corn is washed and soaked in water every day for three or four days. It's then drained and blended with cold water, then blitzed into a smooth consistency. The liquid is separated from the chaff and then left for a few hours to separate from the concentrated corn milk. Finally, some of the water is removed and you're left with ogi! Obviously this is quite a lengthy process, so I wanted to make a cheat's version. To create the distinctively sour taste of ogi, I've used sauerkraut juice.

PREP TIME: 5 MINS
COOKING TIME: 10 MINS
SERVES: 4

100ml sauerkraut juice
125g cornflour or fine
   cornmeal
400ml coconut milk or rice
   milk
50g coconut sugar or caster
   sugar
evaporated milk, to serve
hibiscus petals, to decorate
   (optional)

In a mixing bowl, slowly whisk the sauerkraut juice into the cornflour or cornmeal, removing the lumps as you go along. When everything is well combined, set aside.

Pour the coconut or rice milk and sugar into a saucepan set over a high heat. Stir for 5 minutes, until the sugar dissolves. Bring the pan off the heat and leave to cool for 2 minutes. Add the corn starch liquid into the milk, whisking vigorously. Return the pan to a low heat and continue to whisk for 3 minutes until it becomes thick and custardy.

Best served hot, drizzled with evaporated milk and hibiscus petals (if using). If you're not ready to serve the ogi straight away, pour it into a container and cover with cling film, making sure it comes into contact with the custard, so that no skin forms.

❀ NOTES
If you'd prefer not to use coconut milk, you can substitute water for the milk.

MANGO OGI TART

Mango always brings a smile to my face — partly because it brings back fond memories of my time at boarding school in Nigeria (where the mangoes were always particularly delectable) and partly because of its deliciousness and vibrancy. It's the perfect fruit to pair with ogi — with its intriguing sourness — and combined, these ingredients make a really spectacular pudding to rival your standard custard tart.

PREP TIME: 20 MINS
   PLUS CHILLING TIME
COOKING TIME: 15 MINS
SERVES: 6

FOR THE CRUST
60g coconut flour
160g ground egusi seeds or
   ground almonds
2 tbsp coconut sugar or
   unrefined dark brown sugar
¼ tsp salt
3 tbsp melted coconut oil or
   groundnut oil, plus extra for
   greasing

FOR THE FILLING
160ml coconut cream
340ml mango juice
1 tsp vanilla extract
80g cornflour
80ml sauerkraut juice or
   water
100g caster sugar
1–2 mangoes, sliced

Preheat oven to 160ºC/Gas 3 and lightly oil a 20cm pie tin.

In a large bowl, using your hands, mix the coconut flour, ground egusi seeds, sugar, salt, oil and 60ml water until combined. The mixture will feel slightly sticky but it should hold together. Tip the crust mix into the prepared pie tin and press down to get a flat even layer. Bake for roughly 15 minutes until lightly browned, then let cool completely in the tin.

While the crust cools, bring the coconut cream, mango juice and vanilla to a boil in a small saucepan, then reduce the heat to low. In a separate bowl, mix the cornflour with the sauerkraut juice or water. Pour the cornflour mixture into the pan along with the sugar and stir continuously for 5 minutes until well combined and thickened.

Carefully pour the mango ogi into the pre-baked tart crust, and let it set in the fridge. Once set, arrange the slices of mango over the custard. Divide the pie into 6 slices to serve.

PLANTAIN CRÊPES

I first made these for my family during the Christmas holidays one year. My cousins and I couldn't decide if we wanted fried plantains or crêpes for breakfast, so we decided to experiment with both and the result was a real treat. In true Nigerian style, I've paired the crêpes with a spicy syrup, but this can easily be replaced with chocolate or caramel sauce if you prefer. For extra taste and texture, I sometimes add crispy bacon on top of mine, too.

PREP TIME: 15 MINS
COOKING TIME: 40 MINS
SERVES: 4

2 eggs
200ml almond milk
2 tbsp coconut oil, melted,
    plus extra for greasing
½ tsp vanilla extract
½ yellow plantain, mashed
125g plain flour
3 tbsp unrefined brown sugar
    or coconut sugar

FOR THE CHILLI SYRUP
300ml coconut nectar or
    honey
2cm piece of fresh ginger,
    peeled and chopped
1 tsp cayenne pepper
½ tsp crushed chilli flakes

To make the chilli syrup, add all the ingredients to a saucepan along with 200ml water and bring to the boil. Reduce the heat a little and leave to simmer for 8 minutes, until the syrup has reduced by about half and is glossy. Remove from the heat and leave to cool. If you prefer your syrup without bits in, pass it through a sieve to remove the ginger.

For the batter, gently beat the eggs in a large bowl, then whisk in the almond milk, coconut oil, vanilla extract and mashed plantain until well combined. In another bowl, mix together the flour and sugar. Pour the wet mix into the dry mix a bit at a time, whisking as you go along. Once the batter is smooth and fluid, set aside.

Using kitchen paper, rub coconut oil around a small frying pan to lightly grease it, and place it over a medium heat. (You will need to regrease the pan after every one or two pancakes.) Pour a small ladleful of batter into the centre of the pan and swirl the pan to spread it out thinly and evenly. Cook each crêpe for 2 minutes until the bottom is crispy, flip and cook for a further 2 minutes before removing from the pan. Keep doing this until there is no more batter left. You should be able to make about 8 crêpes.

To serve, fold each crêpe in half and pour over some chilli syrup. Fold the crêpe once more and drizzle over some more.

LAGOS MESS

At boarding school, our families were allowed to visit once a fortnight to take us out for the day. Mine would usually end up taking me to some distant relative's birthday party or wedding. I remember feeling like I was melting in the car because the weather was absolutely boiling and it always took such a long time for Lagos traffic to clear. When we were stuck in an endless queue, vendors on bicycles would approach the car to sell frozen treats. Each had the same things on offer – strawberry yoghurt, vanilla ice cream and chocolate milk. They were sweet, creamy and refreshing, and after a heated argument about which flavour to get, my uncle would thankfully get a bagful to cool everyone down. My take on the British classic Eton mess is inspired by the memories of those welcome treats.

PREP TIME: 25 MINS
SERVES: 4

300ml double cream
seeds from 1 vanilla pod
1 tbsp caster sugar
4 ready-made meringue nests
500g strawberries, hulled
   and sliced
250ml coconut yoghurt or
   Greek yoghurt
50g milk chocolate, grated
100g Coffee Chin Chin
   (page 165), or any coffee
   biscuit, crushed

In a mixing bowl, whip the double cream and vanilla seeds with the sugar until thick but still soft and not grainy at all. Break the meringues into various-sized chunks and stir into the cream.

In another bowl, crush two-fifths of the strawberries with a fork and mix with the coconut or Greek yoghurt.

Divide the meringue and cream mix between four glasses or small bowls, followed by the strawberry mix. Sprinkle over the grated milk chocolate, coffee chin chin and remaining sliced strawberries. Serve immediately.

HIBISCUS POACHED PEARS

I used to think of poached pears as one of those desserts that only really advanced cooks could make, when, in reality, it's something that can be made with little to no training in the kitchen. Pears are the perfect canvas for absorbing flavour. I like to infuse mine with hibiscus, ginger and cloves, as well as uda pods (but these aren't essential), and serve them alongside the creamy coconut yoghurt and rich syrup. The more syrup you pour on, the brighter red the pear becomes. This makes for a really fresh, exciting pudding — not in the slightest bit passé!

PREP TIME: 5 MINS
COOKING TIME: 30 MINS
SERVES: 4

2 uda pods, crushed
  (optional)
2 tbsp fine-cut dried hibiscus
  petals
200g sugar
zest of 2 lemons
4 whole cloves
4cm piece of fresh ginger,
  peeled and grated
2 tbsp fine-cut dried hibiscus
  petals
4 conference pears, peeled
coconut yoghurt or double
  cream, to serve

Put all the ingredients except for the pears into a large saucepan along with 500ml water. Mix together and turn the heat up to high. Once the liquid begins to boil, bring the heat down to low and let simmer for 10 minutes so the flavours can meld together.

Submerge the pears in the hibiscus syrup and cover the pot. Leave the pears to poach gently for about 20 minutes, depending on their ripeness. Test if they are tender by inserting a small sharp knife, and cook for a little longer if it doesn't go in easily. When tender, take the pears from the pan and boil the rest of the liquid to thicken the syrup.

Serve each pear with a drizzle of the syrup and some coconut yoghurt or cream.

GRAPEFRUIT AND GUAVA CHEESECAKE

Ideally, you would use wara in this recipe, which is a cheese eaten by the Fulani and Hausa ethnic groups in Nigeria and is more commonly served as a snack than cooked into a dessert. Mozzarella makes a great substitute though, giving a really rich consistency to this cheesecake. The base uses crushed Chin Chin (see page 164) and the filling is made from guava, for a tropical twist. The slices of grapefruit on top add sweetness and look beautiful. If you're able to get your hands on some, melted guava jam works really well as a sauce to go over the top, but it's not essential. It's a very decadent dessert, perfect for any dinner party.

PREP TIME: 30 MINS PLUS CHILLING AND SETTING
COOKING TIME: 30 MINS
SERVES: 12

200g Traditional Chin Chin (page 164)
100ml groundnut oil
2 tbsp coconut oil
2 tbsp cassava flour or plain flour
150ml rice milk
125g mozzarella cheese, grated
250g mascarpone cheese
100g icing sugar
4 tbsp freshly squeezed lemon juice
2 tsp vanilla extract
410g tin guava halves in syrup, drained
150ml coconut cream
5 gelatine leaves, softened in cold water
2 red grapefruits, peeled and sliced

Line the base and sides of a 23-cm springform cake tin with baking paper.

Using either a food processor or a ziplock bag and a rolling pin, crush the chin chin into coarse crumbs. Transfer the crumbs to a bowl, mix in the groundnut oil and tip into the prepared tin. Press the chin chin mix into the tin, using your fingers or the back of a spoon to create an even layer. Place the tin in the fridge to chill and firm up for at least 30 minutes.

Meanwhile, in a saucepan set over a high heat, melt the coconut oil and whisk in the flour until translucent. Slowly add the rice milk to the wet cassava paste, whisking constantly to avoid any lumps. Turn the heat down to medium–low, add the grated mozzarella and stir for roughly 6 minutes until completely melted and the sauce is creamy.

In a large bowl, beat together the mascarpone, icing sugar, lemon juice and vanilla extract until fluffy. Slowly whisk in the mozzarella sauce until well combined, then set aside.

Blitz the guava halves in a food processor or using a hand-held blender to form a pulp. Pass the pulp through a sieve into a bowl, discarding the seeds, and set aside.

Warm the coconut cream in a small saucepan set over a medium heat for about 5 minutes. Remove the gelatine leaves from the water and squeeze out any excess moisture. Add the leaves to the warmed coconut cream and stir until dissolved.

To complete the filling, add the coconut cream to the cheese mixture, along with the guava pulp and mix until well incorporated and thick. Pour the filling into the biscuit-lined pan and smooth the top using a rubber spatula or back of a spoon Place the cheesecake in the fridge and let chill for at least 4 hours, or overnight, until set.

Carefully remove the cheesecake from the tin and top it with the grapefruit slices. Allow the cheesecake to come to room temperature before cutting into 12 slices to serve.

PLANTAIN ICE CREAM

I must admit that I got this idea from a tweet that went viral some time ago. A man was stood in an American ice-cream parlour holding a tub of vanilla ice cream with fried plantain chunks on top, so I set out on a mission to make my own version. The beauty of plantain is that it is extremely versatile — it does everything a banana can do and more. In this case, it creates a really creamy ice cream with a mellow flavour.

**PREP TIME: 20 MINS
PLUS FREEZING TIME
COOKING TIME: 10 MINS
SERVES: 4–6**

2 yellow plantains, peeled
and sliced
½ tsp vanilla extract
2 tbsp coconut nectar or
honey
1 tsp ground nutmeg
1 tsp ground ginger
100ml coconut cream

FOR THE PLANTAIN SYRUP
1 black plantain, peeled and
finely chopped
120g coconut sugar or
unrefined brown sugar

TO SERVE
2 tbsp carob powder
4 tbsp peanuts or cashew
nuts, roughly chopped

Put the yellow plantains into a ziplock bag and store them in the freezer for about 4 hours, or overnight, until frozen solid.

Meanwhile, in a small saucepan over a medium–high heat, combine the black plantain and sugar and cook for 6–8 minutes until caramelized and golden. Add 60ml water, stir, then bring to the boil. Cook for a couple of minutes until the plantain is completely broken down and the mixture is smooth, then remove from the heat and set aside to cool.

Blitz the frozen plantains in a food processor until smooth, then add the vanilla extract, coconut nectar or honey, nutmeg, ginger and coconut cream. Whizz for a further minute until everything is well combined.

Pour alternate layers of the ice cream and syrup into a 1lb loaf tin or a 500ml plastic container. Use a toothpick to marble the plantain syrup through the ice cream, then cover with cling film and put in the freezer for at least 1 hour to firm up.

Take the ice cream out of the freezer 15 minutes or so before serving so that it is easy to scoop. During that time, gather your serving ingredients. Scoop the ice cream into bowls, dust with carob powder and top with the chopped nuts.

✿ **NOTES**
You could swap the peanuts or cashews for macadamias, almonds or any other nuts you might have in the cupboard, if you like.

PEANUT POPCORN

Popcorn is such an intensely satisfying snack in so many ways. It's super quick (which is essential as far as I'm concerned) but I also love the sound the kernels make in the pan – frenzied at first and then more sporadic until they're all puffed and ready. I know lots of people like sweet or toffee popcorn but this spicy, nutty version is a must-try.

PREP TIME: 5 MINS
COOKING TIME: 5 MINS
MAKES: 4 VERY LARGE BOWLS

5 tbsp groundnut oil
200g popping corn kernels
1 tbsp roasted peanut flour
4 tbsp peanuts, chopped
salt and cayenne pepper

Using a large stock pan, heat 4 tablespoons of the groundnut oil over a medium–high heat. After about 1 minute, check the oil is hot enough by adding 2 or 3 kernels of corn to the pan. The oil is ready once the kernels pop. Add the rest of the popcorn and cover with a lid. Continuously shake the pan back and forth while over the heat, and once the rate of popping slows to a 6-second gap between pops, remove the pan from the heat. Carefully take off the lid as some kernels might still pop, and transfer the popcorn to a large bowl.

Mix the last tablespoon of groundnut oil and the peanut flour together. Add to the bowl of popcorn along with the chopped peanuts and mix until well coated. Season to taste with salt and cayenne pepper.

Serve warm.

MADAM KOIN KOIN

I'm not sure what it is about boarding schools and ghost stories, but it seems no matter where you are in the world they all have one. Madam Koin Koin is a ghost said to walk around in red shoes, which can be heard echoing through hallways. Like a lot of Yoruba words, the name given to something is based on the sound it makes, in this instance 'koin koin'. So, as I'm not superstitious, I thought it would be fun to make a brittle that mimics that sound and the colour of Madam Koin Koin's heels.

PREP TIME: 5 MINS
   PLUS COOLING TIME
COOKING TIME: 10 MINS
SERVES: 12

oil, for greasing
200g flaked almonds or egusi
   seeds
200g caster sugar
150ml corn syrup
2 drops red food
   colouring (optional)

Grease a baking tray with butter or oil and line it with baking paper.

In a small dry frying pan over a medium heat, toast the almonds until they start to turn golden brown. (If you are using egusi seeds, toast them until they begin to pop). Spread the almonds or egusi seeds out on the tray in a thin, even layer.

In a saucepan set over a medium heat, combine the sugar, corn syrup and 120ml water. Stir until the sugar has dissolved, then bring the syrup to the boil and boil for roughly 5 minutes, or until a dark caramel colour. Add the red food colouring, if using, and stir until well combined. Carefully tip the liquid all over the almonds or egusi seeds and leave for 30 minutes to cool and harden.

When the brittle is cool enough to handle, shatter into pieces by hitting it with a spoon and enjoy. If you're not planning on eating them straight away, store the pieces in an airtight container.

MANGO AND COCONUT PARFAIT

The parfait here is made in the American way, seeing as there is no frozen cream or yoghurt but just a layering up of delicious ingredients. The zesty lemon of the Chin Chin complements the creaminess of the coconut whip and the mango cubes saturated with a sweet syrup. Once layered on top of each other, the syrup soaks into the chin chin (although not so much as to make them go soggy), creating an eruption of bliss in your mouth. I've included tarragon in my recipe because its delicate aroma really brings the dish together — herbs aren't just for savoury dishes!

PREP TIME: 20 MINS PLUS COOLING TIME
COOKING TIME: 10 MINS
SERVES: 4

4cm piece of fresh ginger, peeled and diced
150g jam sugar
2 tbsp finely chopped tarragon, plus extra to serve
2 mangoes, peeled, pitted and finely chopped
250ml double cream
2 tsp vanilla extract
175ml coconut yoghurt or Greek yoghurt
240g Lemon Chin Chin (page 166) or any lemon biscuit

Put the ginger and sugar in a saucepan with 200ml water and bring to the boil, then reduce the heat to low and let simmer for roughly 10 minutes until the mixture begins to thicken. Take the ginger syrup off the heat, add the tarragon and let sit for 5–10 minutes to infuse the flavours. Sieve the syrup into a bowl to remove the leaves and ginger, then let sit for roughly 15 minutes to cool down. Spoon a little of the diced mango into a separate small bowl and set aside in the fridge, for decorating. Gently mix the remaining mango into the syrup and put in the fridge to chill.

Meanwhile, whip the cream until stiff peaks form. In a separate large bowl, gently mix the vanilla extract into the yoghurt. A bit at a time, fold the whipped cream into the yoghurt until fluffy. Keep in the fridge until ready to assemble.

Crush the chin chin into crumbs by blitzing in a food processor or by placing inside a ziplock bag and bashing using a rolling pin. Cover and set aside in a dry area.

When ready to assemble, gather four glass cups. Spoon 3–4 tablespoons of the crushed chin chin into each cup, followed by 3 tablespoons of the mango in syrup, and finally 3 tablespoons of the cream mix. Repeat for a second time to layer up the glasses, then top with the reserved mango and a sprinkling of tarragon.

INDEX

CONVERSION CHARTS

DRY WEIGHTS

METRIC	IMPERIAL
5g	¼oz
8/10g	⅓oz
15g	½oz
20g	¾oz
25g	1oz
30/35g	1¼oz
40g	1½oz
50g	2oz
60/70g	2½oz
75/85/90g	3oz
100g	3½oz
110/120g	4oz
125/130g	4½oz
135/140/150g	5oz
170/175g	6oz
200g	7oz
225g	8oz
250g	9oz
265g	9½oz
275g	10oz
300g	11oz
325g	11½oz
350g	12oz
375g	13oz
400g	14oz
425g	15oz
450g	1lb
475g	1lb 1oz
500g	1lb 2oz
550g	1lb 3oz
600g	1lb 5oz
625g	1lb 6oz
650g	1lb 7oz
675g	1½lb
700g	1lb 9oz
750g	1lb 10oz
800g	1¾lb
850g	1lb 14oz
900g	2lb
950g	2lb 2oz
1kg	2lb 3oz
1.1kg	2lb 6oz
1.25kg	2¾lb
1.3/1.4kg	3lb
1.5kg	3lb 5oz
1.75/1.8kg	4lb

LIQUID MEASURES

568ml = 1 UK pint (20fl oz)
16fl oz = 1 US pint

METRIC	IMPERIAL	CUPS / TBSP
15ml	½fl oz	1 tbsp (level)
20ml	¾fl oz	
25ml	1fl oz	⅛ cup
30ml	1¼fl oz	
50ml	2fl oz	¼ cup
60ml	2½fl oz	
75ml	3fl oz	
100ml	3½fl oz	⅜ cup
110/120ml	4fl oz	½ cup
125ml	4½fl oz	
150ml	5fl oz	⅔ cup
175ml	6fl oz	¾ cup
200/215ml	7fl oz	
225ml	8fl oz	1 cup
250ml	9fl oz	
275ml	9½fl oz	
300ml	½ pint	1¼ cups
350ml	12fl oz	1½ cups
375ml	13fl oz	
400ml	14fl oz	
425ml	15fl oz	
450ml	16fl oz	2 cups
500ml	18fl oz	2¼ cups
550ml	19fl oz	
600ml	1 pint	2½ cups
700ml	1¼ pints	
750ml	1⅓ pints	
800ml	1 pint 9fl oz	
850ml	1½ pints	
900ml	1 pint 12fl oz	3¾ cups
1 litre	1¾ pints	1 US quart (4 cups)

OVEN TEMPERATURES

°C	°F	GAS MARK	DESCRIPTION
110	225	¼	cool
130	250	½	cool
140	275	1	very low
150	300	2	very low
160/170	325	3	low to moderate
180	350	4	moderate
190	375	5	moderately hot
200	400	6	hot
220	425	7	hot
230	450	8	hot
240	475	9	very hot

All recipes are based on fan-assisted oven temperatures. If you are using a conventional oven, raise the temperature 20°C higher than stated in recipes.

ACKNOWLEDGEMENTS

I can't put into words how grateful I am to have been given the chance to write a cookbook. I'm especially grateful to the people around me – without them, this book wouldn't exist nor would the ideas for some recipes have been possible.

To my family, most especially my mother and cousins (Lola, Bolaji and Tolani), thank you for being my biggest supporters and my best friends.

To Abigail, Claud Williams and Marion, thank you for your kind words and advice, and for encouraging me to step out of my comfort zone.

To HDPL group and the Heathcoat Squad for making the most boring of days bubbly with your banter and energy.

To Sam aka Squirrel, thank you for being there to calm me down when deadlines were closing in.

To the *Red* magazine competition judging panel – Pip McCormac, Leslie Leigh, Ronke Lawal, Jessica Laditan, Grace Cheetham and Henna Zamurd-Butt –thank you for seeing my potential and giving me a chance to share my stories and love for food.

To Ellis Parrinder, Laurie Perry and Hannah Wilkinson – the amazing team who brought my food to life – thank you for paying attention to the smallest of details and working rigorously to get the perfect shot.

To Grace Cheetham, Zoe Berville, Sarah Hammond, Mic Alcaino, James Empringham, Polly Osborn, Isabel Prodger, Jasmine Gordon and Orlando Mowbray – thank you for your patience and guidance throughout this process. I've learnt and grown a lot in a short amount of time and feel incredibly lucky to be included in the HarperCollins family.